T3-BNT-459

PERGAMON INTERNATIONAL LIBRARY
of Science, Technology, Engineering and Social Studies
The 1000-volume original paperback library in aid of education,
industrial training and the enjoyment of leisure
Publisher: Robert Maxwell, M.C.

Children with Specific Learning Difficulties

SECOND EDITION

_____Publisher's Notice to Educators_____

THE PERGAMON TEXTBOOK
INSPECTION COPY SERVICE

An inspection copy service of any book published in the Pergamon International
Library will gladly be sent without obligation for consideration for course adoption
or recommendation. Copies may be retained for a period of 60 days from receipt and
returned if not suitable. When a particular title is adopted or recommended for
adoption for class use and the recommendation results in a sale of 12 or more
copies, the inspection copy may be retained with our compliments. If after examination the lecturer decides that the book is not suitable for adoption but would like to
retain it for his personal library, then our Educators' Discount of 10% is allowed on
the invoiced price. The Publishers will be pleased to receive suggestions for revised
editions and new titles to be published in this important International Library.

OTHER TITLES OF INTEREST

BARANYAY, E. P.
The Mentally Handicapped Adolescent

BOYLE, D. G.
A Student's Guide to Piaget

BRUCE, V.
Awakening the Slower Mind

FRANCIS-WILLIAMS, J.
Rorschach with Children

FROMMER, E. A.
Voyage through Childhood into the Adult World

HELMORE, G. A.
Piaget: A Practical Consideration

HERRMANN, E. R. and CAMPBELL, S. F.
Piaget—Dictionary of Terms

LIEBERT, R. M. *et al.*
The Early Window: Effects of TV on Children and Youth

RAVENETTE, A. T.
Dimensions of Reading Difficulties

RENFREW, C. E.
Speech Disorders in Children

SEGAL, S. S.
No Child is Ineducable, 2nd Edition

WING, L.
Early Childhood Autism, 2nd Edition

Children with Specific Learning Difficulties

THE EFFECT OF NEURODEVELOPMENTAL LEARNING DISORDERS ON CHILDREN OF NORMAL INTELLIGENCE

SECOND EDITION

BY

JESSIE FRANCIS-WILLIAMS

*Research Psychologist, Newcomen Centre for Handicapped Children,
Guy's Hospital, London
and lately Consultant Psychologist, Guy's Hospital*

*Formerly Senior Psychologist, Hospital for Sick Children,
Great Ormond Street, London*

*Sometime Psychologist, University College Hospital, London
and Lecturer, University College, London*

PERGAMON PRESS

OXFORD · NEW YORK · TORONTO
SYDNEY · PARIS · FRANKFURT

U. K.	Pergamon Press Ltd., Headington Hill Hall, Oxford OX3 0BW, England
U. S. A.	Pergamon Press Inc., Maxwell House, Fairview Park, Elmsford, New York 10523, U.S.A.
C A N A D A	Pergamon of Canada Ltd., 207 Queen's Quay West, Toronto 1, Canada
A U S T R A L I A	Pergamon Press (Aust.) Pty. Ltd., 19a Boundary Street, Rushcutters Bay, N.S.W. 2011, Australia
F R A N C E	Pergamon Press SARL, 24 rue des Ecoles, 75240 Paris, Cedex 05, France
WEST GERMANY	Pergamon Press GmbH, 6242, Kronberg-Tanus, Pferdstrasse 1, Frankfurt-am-Main, West Germany

First edition 1970

Second edition 1974

Reprinted 1976

Library of Congress Cataloging in Publication Data

Williams, Jessie, Lady Francis-Williams
Children with specific learning difficulties.
(Mental health and social medicine)
Bibliography: p.
1. Brain-damaged children—Education. I. Title.
[DNLM: 1. Learning disorders. 2. Nervous system diseases—In infancy and childhood.   LC4661 F819c 1974]
RJ486.W55   1974   371.9'2   74-4021
ISBN 0 08 017967 3
ISBN 0 08 017968 1 (flexicover)

Printed in Great Britain by A. Wheaton & Co., Exeter

Contents

PREFACE   vii

ACKNOWLEDGEMENTS   ix

Chapter 1. Scope of this Study   1

Chapter 2. Early Learning   16

Chapter 3. A Research Study into the Early Identifi-   30
              cation of Pre-school Children likely to have
              Specific Learning Disorders

Chapter 4. Helping Children Before Starting Formal   75
              School

Chapter 5. Children in School   104

Chapter 6. Experiments in Teaching Children with   142
              Specific Learning Difficulties

Chapter 7. The Outlook for the Future   167

Chapter 8. Results from a Follow-up of Children   175
              studied at 3 to 4 years of age (described in
              Chapter 3)

HISTORICAL SURVEY   192

BIBLIOGRAPHY   212

INDEX   223

Preface

THIS book contains a report of original research into the possibility of early identification of children of normal intelligence, but with specific learning disorders believed to arise from neuro-developmental dysfunction. It is hoped that the results of this research will be of practical value to psychologists and others concerned in the identification and help of such children and the book as a whole has been planned as a practical guide to work in this field. In order to identify deviant development, it is necessary to have an understanding of normal development of learning in young children, and after a preliminary chapter setting out the scope of the work, this is therefore examined, before turning to the research study itself.

The research study, as already stated, was concerned with the identification of difficulties in pre-school children and after reporting on this research, methods of helping pre-school children are then examined.

There follows a consideration of the identification of difficulties in school children and a survey of teaching experiments likely to be of value in helping such children. It is hoped that this approach may prove to be of practical value. Problems for the future are then considered.

An historical survey bringing together and collating research on different aspects of learning disorders is published at the end of the book.

This book was prompted by work over many years with cerebral palsied children and by concern for the specific learning difficulties created by cerebral damage. I have been in a position to follow through to adolescence many children first known to me in pre-school years and to note the extent to which wide discrepancies in their levels of functioning, already plain in early school days, have persisted throughout the whole of their school lives, so that the development of their visuo-spatial ability and their language ability ran, as it were, on separate tracks which never converged.

Seeing these same children in their teens, after their years of battling with such discrepancies in their levels of learning achievement, made me ask whether they might not have been helped more successfully if more had been understood of their ways of learning. As a result of my interest in these children, I began to study similar kinds of learning disability among children who were not physically handicapped, as were those cerebral palsied children with whose learning problems I had become so familiar. Many, although not all of these children with comparable learning disabilities, but without gross physical handicap, were clumsy and inco-ordinated. Some, but not all, had a history of difficult birth, with the possibility of slight organic impairment at birth. Although their problems were not such as to require special educational provision, in the sense of the children listed as "Handicapped Pupils" by the Department of Education, their unusual learning difficulties, if not appreciated by their teachers, did create pressures which militated against successful school experience.

It seemed to me that it was worth inquiry as to whether it might be possible to detect such children in their pre-school years, and if so, what means could be found to help them before their formal schooling began and so enable their actual school years to be happier and more constructive. The research, described in detail in Chapter 3 and discussed at various other points throughout this book, resulted from the interest thus aroused and will, I hope, be found to make some contribution to this problem. It was made possible by a grant from the Spastics' Society, to whom I am much indebted.

Acknowledgements

MY THANKS are due to the University of Illinois Press and Dr. McCarthy and Dr. Kirk for allowing me to reproduce items from the experimental edition of their Psycholinguistics Test, to the Society for Research in Child Development for permission to reprint Dr. Frances Graham's Copy Forms Test, to Dr. Marianne Frostig for permission to reproduce items from her Develop-mental Test of Visual Perception, the American Ortho-psychiatric Association and Dr. Lauretta Bender for the illustration of the Bender Gestalt Test, Dr. Lila Ghent and the *American Journal of Psychology* for permission to reprint figures which illustrate her work.

I am grateful also to Dr. Moya Tyson for illustrations of her "play-exercises" material.

I owe a particular debt of gratitude to Dr. Joan Reynell for going through the manuscript and making a number of most constructive comments and also for allowing me to publish illustrations from her test.

Professor Sir Cyril Burt also kindly read the manuscript and gave me stimulating advice on a number of important points, for which I am most grateful. I owe much also to the consistent interest and encouragement shown by Dr. Mary Wilson, Staff Inspector for Special Education, Inner London Education Authority.

The research described in Chapter 3 would not have been possible without the co-operation of Dr. Stephen Macoun, St. Luke's Hospital, Guildford, Dr. Ronald MacKeith, Director, Handicapped Children's Centre, Newcomen House, Guy's Hospital, London and Dr. Neil O'Doherty, formerly of Guy's Hospital now at West Middlesex Hospital, London; to my research assistant, Staff Nurse Joyce and to Mr. William Yule of the Institute of Education and the Institute of Psychiatry, London who gave invaluable assistance with the statistics.

It is impossible to refer by name to the many colleagues who have given generously of their time in discussing aspects of this work and in doing so have helped to clarify my ideas. I cannot, however, let this book go into print without expressing my deep obligation to Dr. Mary Sheridan, then at Newcomen Centre, for her wisdom and rare insight into children's problems and for her practical help where there were complications of vision, hearing or speech affecting some of the children in this study. Her interest and enthusiasm sustained me during those periods, which all research workers will know, when it seemed impossible to see any light at the end of the tunnel.

Finally, I must thank my Secretary, Mrs. Irene Jackson, who has helped me far beyond the line of secretarial duty, and my husband, who has met all the slings and arrows of my preoccupation with unshaken good humour.

I am grateful to Mrs. Ducker, Senior Editor of Pergamon Press, who has been unfailingly helpful in the preparation of this book.

The follow-up described in Chapter 8 was made possible by a further grant from the Spastics Society

CHAPTER 1

Scope of this Study

THIS book is concerned with special categories of children whose level of achievement in certain school subjects is not up to the standard of their overall intelligence. Children do badly in school for many reasons. They may have low intelligence. They may have had poor opportunities and have received little encouragement at home. They may have sensory deficits, particularly of vision and hearing, or physical handicaps which seriously impair their learning. They may be secretly wrestling with problems of emotional relationships that drain off mental energy and divert it from the task in hand, so that they day-dream instead of concentrating. They may already have failed in school and be battling with the emotional effects of their failure. All these conditions can be recognized and when they are recognized, the children can receive appropriate help.

The concern here, however, is with children whose difficulties in school learning are associated with and apparently caused by disturbances in maturation, or by organic neurological impairment. Many terms have been used to describe these children— "brain-injured" or "brain-damaged" children, "neurologically handicapped" children, children with "minimal cerebral dysfunction." Myklebust (1964) defines specific learning disabilities as the result of minor disturbances of brain function and he suggests the use of the term "psychoneurological" to indicate that such disabilities are the psychological concomitants of neurological deficits. After much consideration, it was decided here to use the term "neurodevelopmental" learning disorders because, although many of the children were identified by psychological tests as having specific learning disorders similar to those of children with known neurological impairment, there is no evidence of such impairment in some of these children. However, there is frequently evidence of maturational lag and disorderly development that needs to be recognized in planning suitable learning programmes to prevent specific learning disabilities becoming fixed.

The causes of this kind of school failure are often not so readily apparent. Nevertheless if they go unrecognized, they inevitably create for the child the kind of anxiety and stress that follows from frustration and failure. Often, the special difficulties of these children are not recognized until they have started school and are already falling behind in school work. It is then that teachers may ask for advice and help from the school medical officer or school psychologist. Parents, on the other hand, may seek help from the family doctor, because they are worried about anomalies of development and behaviour during the pre-school period or because their child is not doing as well at school as they had hoped.

A full investigation of such cases calls for a team approach. However, this book is not concerned with the paediatric or neurological aspects of such investigations. The latter are fully covered in *The Neurological Examination of Children* by Paine and Oppé (1966). The present aim is rather to facilitate by description, the recognition of these children by psychologists and to increase the understanding by those school doctors and teachers of the difficulties that arise for them.

Writing of these children Paine (1965) describes them as showing "irregularly impaired cerebral function usually referred to as an 'organic pattern' which could conceivably exist as a uniform disability in different areas of function but which usually shows striking discrepancies from one area to another". And, he continues, "these are the difficulties which often constitute the principal barrier to academic performance in children with cerebral palsies or epilepsy and which can also exist by themselves in a borderline or [almost] 'subclinical' form".

It is these "borderline" cases with which we are concerned here. For convenience, they will be discussed under two heads:

1. Children whose learning disabilities arise,
   (a) from poor and disorderly development of visual perception,
   (b) from poor motor co-ordination, as a result of which their visuo-motor skills are poor and they are handicapped in many areas of learning.
2. Children whose learning disabilities arise from language disorders,
   (a) caused by some degree of auditory imperception, or handicap in speech arising from developmental dysphasia, either receptive, expressive or both,
   (b) resulting from developmental dyslexia—the term currently used for very severe reading difficulty thought to have a genetic origin.

The overlap between these conditions is considerable and, unless the child's condition and its cause is recognized and concessions are made, both at home and school, there will inevitably be severe emotional disorders which may further confuse the diagnosis.

Although for the sake of clarity these two categories are discussed separately, it will be shown that in many ways, all areas of development are affected and contribute to the disability in learning. They have been chosen for discussion because the learning difficulties that arise are believed to be due basically either to congenital conditions causing maturational delay, or to cerebral damage at birth or in early infancy.

1. Children whose Learning Difficulties Arise from Poor and Disorderly Development of Visual Perception and Poor Visuo-motor Skills

Knowledge of the world we live in is gained primarily through our senses, sight, hearing and, particularly for young children, touch. What we see or hear or feel, however, must be perceived, that is interpreted and given meaning. Strauss (1947), a pioneer in finding methods of teaching brain injured children, defined perception as "the mental process which gives particular meaning and significance to a given sensation and therefore acts as a preliminary to thinking. It is the means by which the individual organises and comes to understand the phenomena which constantly impinge upon him."

In the early learning stages, visual perception plays a very important part. Years of careful experimentation by such workers as Fantz (1966) in America have shown that the very young infant views selectively those patterns that have intrinsic interest for him. Very early, he demonstrates his preferential interest in the kinds of form that will later help in recognition of objects and in spatial orientation. This visual experience contributes to early learning and leads the young child to explore objects, combining touch and movement to extend his visual experience.

Over the past two decades, workers with cerebral palsied children have become increasingly aware that some of them have learning difficulties more severe than might be accounted for by their motor and sensory handicaps. These difficulties, many of which are thought to arise from deviant or delayed development of visual perception and consequent related difficulty in visuo-motor tasks, have been noted and discussed in most recent books on cerebral palsy and its various facets. They are referred to by psychologists in surveys such as those by Dunsdon (1951) and Floyer (1953) and in such accounts of cerebral palsy as those by Woods (1956), Cardwell (1956), Illingworth (1958), Denhoff and Robinault (1960) and Holt and Reynell (1967).

The special learning difficulties that are to be discussed here arise from: (a) visual perceptual disorders, which do not necessarily correlate with peripheral defects of vision such as would be diagnosed by the ophthalmologist and (b) visuo-motor disorders, where the child's difficulty lies in carrying out motor tasks which require visual control or guidance. It is important to recognize the distinction between these two areas of difficulty, even though many damaged children have disorders in both perceptual and visuo-motor tasks—that is, in both perception and manipulation of spatial relationships; the term "visuo-spatial" is used here to cover both disorders in perception and in manipulation of spatial relationships.

Disorders in visual perception are seen in difficulties in recognizing shapes and patterns, matching blocks according to their shape and size. The kind of task such as "Recognition of Forms" which occurs at the $4\frac{1}{2}$ year level in the Stanford–Binet test has often proved insuperably difficult for very much older cerebral palsied children who are normally intelligent in many areas of functioning. Children with visuo-perceptual disorders have difficulty in recognizing position and distinguishing figure from background in interpreting pictures and, indeed, in orientating themselves in space. These children find it difficult to get meaning from two-dimensional pictures and to relate them to the three-dimensional object which they represent.

When perceptual abilities are required for visuo-motor or constructional tasks, the effect on learning for children with disordered perception is often very damaging. This is seen in the difficulties these children experience in learning to read, to recognize and reproduce letters and words, to write, and to set down on paper a simple sum, which requires that units are put in a column beneath each other and the tens below the tens.

While it is generally accepted that chronological age and its concomitant level of maturation and also general intelligence are important factors in determining the level of perceptual ability in the child, it is also clear that perceptual distortions and consequent specific learning disabilities, such as are seen in some cerebral palsied children, are due to organic impairment. From her study of a city's cerebral palsied children, Floyer (1955) formed the opinion that there is a strong element of developmental lag in the perceptual handicaps of these children. Both Nielsen (1962) and Wedell (1960a) found visuo-motor retardation most marked in the younger children and noted a slow but gradual improvement over the school years. This writer (1968), in a study of the development of a severely spastic girl from 11 to 18 years of age, found a definite, though limited, improvement in her visual perceptual ability, as evidenced through her response to the Rorschach.

Localization and Extent of Brain Damage in Differing Types of Cerebral Palsy

Several attempts have been made to relate the results obtained in perceptual and visuo-motor studies to the various types of cerebral palsy. Many investigators—Cruickshank *et al.* (1957), Bortner and Birch (1962), Abercrombie *et al.* (1964)—found that athetoids performed better than spastics of the same age and I.Q. in visuo-spatial tests. As a result of a carefully designed sub-division of his sample of cerebral palsied children, Wedell (1960a and b) showed that differences existed, not only between athetoids and spastics, but also that spastics with a bilateral motor defect and spastics with left-sided hemiplegia obtained significantly poorer results than the right-sided hemiplegics and the athetoids. This finding of disorder in left hemiplegics but not in right hemiplegics has been disputed by many other workers (Woods, 1957).

Although most workers agree that athetoids tend to have less perceptual and visuo-motor impairment than spastics, there are some who do not. Drawing from her study of the educability of cerebral palsied children, which was based on 3700 boys and girls ranging in age from birth to the end of their sixteenth year, Dunsdon (1951) says that in tasks involving spatial orientation and judgement, athetoids are far more handicapped than are spastics. Floyer (1955) found no clear relationship of visuo-spatial disorder to type of cerebral palsy.

Many of the conclusions arrived at up to the present can only be regarded as tentative and awaiting further research. There is still conflict among clinicians in placing children with cerebral palsy into well-defined categories, so that it is as yet difficult to relate functional disorders to the site of the brain lesion in children as workers such as Wedell have tried to do.

Writing of perceptual disorders found in some cerebral palsied children, Denhoff and Robinault (1960) say: "True perceptual disorders are always of organic origin but this is not to say that they are irremediable. If therapeutic measures are begun during pre-school years, these disorders may be corrected. If treatment is delayed until the age of 6, 8 or later, they may be straightened out but meanwhile confuse regular school learning." Unless they are detected early and help is given, "disturbances which may seriously affect the overall development of the individual may become established, rather than corrected during the formative period when they are most remediable".

So far, research has not yet demonstrated the extent to which these conditions are in themselves remediable. Nevertheless it is the concern of the doctor, the psychologist and the teacher that they should be recognized early, so that ways can be found to help the child to compensate for the disabilities thus caused.

As early as 1947, Strauss and his co-workers pointed out the similarity between some cerebral palsied children and children whom he described as "brain-injured", though not physically handicapped as are cerebral palsied children. "It is now beginning to be recognized," he maintained, "that behaviour and learning may be affected by minimal brain injuries without apparent lowering of the intelligence level."

The work of Strauss and his colleagues was directed towards finding ways of educating these so-called brain-injured children so that they could compensate for their special intellectual deficits.

Behaviour Patterns of Children with Perceptual Disorders

In his plan for helping these children, Strauss placed great emphasis on the difficulties arising from figure–ground disturbance. He saw in this an explanation of the restlessness and distracti-bility of these children. He held that those children whose cerebral damage made it difficult for them to distinguish figure from back-ground have difficulty also in concentrating on what is significant for them at the time and are consequently distracted by all the varying sights and sounds that impinge on their senses. These children cannot easily keep their thinking in focus and they find it difficult to construct and retain a stable perceptual world. Because certain kinds of difficulty in learning and thought processes were frequently associated with hyper-active restless behaviour, short attention span and excessive distractibility, it was but a short step to the assumption that certain patterns of disordered behaviour were in themselves evidence of organic neurological impairment.

In a letter to the editor of the *Cerebral Palsy Bulletin*, Pond (1960) deplored the increasing use that was being made of a general diagnosis of "brain damage" to cover a variety of symptoms, found together in children attending child guidance clinics. He listed the symptoms commonly said to be typical of brain damage as over-activity or hyperkinesis, distractibility and short attention span, lability of mood, anti-social behaviour, low intelligence with characteristic anomalies in sub-test scores and anxiety of a particularly intense degree, leading to catastrophic reaction. He claimed that any single one of the symptoms, or several in combination, might be seen in children who have no evidence of brain injury in their history or in the results of careful investigations and he further claimed that "apart from the symptoms that arise directly from the *loss* of brain function, chronic disorders following brain damage are largely the result of mishandling of the child by parents and society generally".

This view has been disputed by many paediatricians and psychiatrists. Stone (1961) held that:

> certain of these children show a form of impaired ego control which causes them to react to stress in an extreme and characteristic fashion. In cases where there are gross perceptual defects this, I believe, has a direct bearing on subsequent distortions of personality development— for example, as a result of misinterpretation of reality experiences from infancy onwards.

Naturally, it is primarily this behavioural aspect of the possible effects of brain damage on children that interests psychiatrists.

The real contribution made by Strauss, however, was to demonstrate that suitable methods of teaching children whose cerebral damage had caused anomalies of intellectual functioning were in themselves a form of therapy. This improved personality and emotional adjustment, and indeed the child's total pattern of behaviour.

Strauss and his colleagues were concerned to develop ways of helping those brain-injured children who showed disturbances in visuo-spatial perception, disturbed orientation in regard to structure, shape and size, and other defects thought to be related to perceptual disorders which could not entirely be accounted for by the disorders of movement, nor entirely related to such physical disabilities as deafness, total or partial defective vision, squints, defective speech, epilepsy and general low intelligence.

Although these perceptual disorders create many learning problems for the children with cerebral palsy who suffer them, similar malfunction has been recognized in children who are not cerebral palsied. This group of children has been described by Illingworth (1964) as "clumsy children", or children with "minimal cerebral palsy". He says, "It is obvious that there are all grades of severity of cerebral palsy varying from the severely spastic, totally incapacitated patient to the most trivial and truly minimal one", among which he would place this particular group of "clumsy children". It is generally recognized by paediatricians and paediatric neurologists that children can be found with minimal or no spasticity, but who show marked disturbance of other functions of the brain, which are now known to be frequently present in children showing obvious spasticity.

It is important that psychologists should not fail to recognize these children when help or advice is sought. On the other hand, it is equally important that a child should not be lightly diagnosed as "brain injured" when the problem is one of slow or disturbed normal development. This distinction between slow normal development and anomalous development due to possible brain pathology can be extremely difficult to make. The younger the child, the more difficult it is to make a clear diagnosis because the range of normal development of some of the skills known to be sensitive to brain pathology is very wide indeed and it is also extremely difficult to distinguish in young children the effects of emotional relationships and stimulation within the home from the effect of maturation on the development of such skills.

When we are dealing with children whose medical history is known—hydrocephalics, epileptics, or those who have had lobectomies or head injuries caused by accidents—we are aware of possibilities of damage and can, by careful observation and testing, more readily assess cerebral deficits in the child. But it is much more difficult to detect so-called minimal cerebral palsy cases and to decide whether the learning difficulties which they frequently show are due to organic neurological impairment which is likely to be permanent. If so, ways will have to be found by which the child can compensate for the disabilities in learning which this creates for him.

While stressing that no two children are alike in the extent and severity of the damage they have suffered, it is the writer's experience that the following characteristics, in varying combinations, would suggest that we are dealing with a child whose developmental lag and learning problems in school are due to brain pathology and not to normal slow development in children of school age.

1. Discrepant psychological test patterning: for example, in the Wechsler Pre-school and Primary Scale of Intelligence and also in the Wechsler Intelligence Scale for Children, facility in language, difficulty in block design, object assembly and coding and frequently poor arithmetic.
2. Poor school achievement in reading, spelling and writing, compared with the overall Verbal I.Q.
3. Difficulty in right–left discrimination.
4. Clumsiness in movement—games, running, catching balls and in fine motor co-ordination, such as is required in using a knife and fork or in clear speech articulation.
5. Difficulty in dressing, buttoning coat, tying shoes and bows.
6. Loss of figure–ground discrimination in pictures or in reality.
7. Disturbed orientation.

8. Difficulty in copying, recognizing and matching shapes and structures.
9. Psychological disturbances usually associated with cerebral palsy, e.g. perseveration, short attention span, distractibility, fluctuation in performance.
10. Disturbance of body image, e.g. difficulty in relating one part of the body to another.

These are the children classified by some paediatricians and neurologists as "clumsy children" or "children with minimal cerebral palsy". Their difficulties in learning the basic school subjects, reading and number, arise mainly from delayed or distorted development of spatial ability—that is, disorders in both perception and the manipulation of spatial relationships.

2. Children with Language Disorders

Spoken language is the readiest means of communication of ideas and thoughts between people. It has been described as a threefold process. First, there is the reception of a sensory stimulus. This is followed by the intellectual process of interpretation of the meaning of the stimulus. Finally, there is the expression of the response, which ends in the motor activity of speech.

There are many reasons why a child may fail to develop intelligible speech. The most obvious possible cause may be deafness. Children who in the early crucial years for language development have suffered severe emotional deprivation also show delayed development in the use of language very frequently. This is shown vividly in studies of severely deprived children, e.g. *Children Reared in Institutions from Infancy* (Williams, 1961). Many young autistic children do not communicate in speech at all. Retarded language development is also in some cases a concomitant of mental defect. Many children with cerebral palsy also suffer from paralysis or inco-ordination of the muscles involved in articulation. This creates delay and difficulty in use of speech. A number of children, not obviously cerebral palsied,

also have disorders of articulatory mechanisms. These "dysarthric" children have faulty pronunciation of certain sounds or
groups of sounds, predominantly consonants. This may be
caused by spastic weakness of the muscles of articulation, from
interference by involuntary movements with their normal co-
ordination or from ataxia due to cerebellar deficiency. Whatever
the cause, poor articulation very frequently creates for the child
difficulty in many areas of learning, particularly in learning to
read.

There are also some children who have delayed language
development or delay in adequate use of speech, while their
development in other respects is normal. It is this group of children and the learning difficulties that arise for them that are to be
discussed in this study.

Ingram (1964) classifies the speech disorders of these children
as the "developmental speech disorder syndrome". Children in
this category suffer from specific retardation of speech development which cannot be attributed to co-existent disease or adverse
environmental factors. He shows that these children often have a
high incidence of family history of slow speech development. He
includes among them children suffering from auditory imperception, word deafness and central deafness, or so-called developmental receptive and expressive dysphasia.

In her discussion of delayed development of speech Morley
(1965) defines developmental dysphasia as a condition in which
"development of speech is delayed beyond the range of what is
normal, and the child's ability to formulate his thoughts into
words and sentences is inadequate for his age". She holds that
"this condition may be associated with cerebral palsy or exist in
the absence of any obvious underlying neurological disorder and
may possibly be the result of some critical agenesis or dysfunction
producing delay in the acquisition of the use of the audible symbols of speech".

In adults, aphasia is the term used for a defect in symbolic
language due to cerebral pathology. Aphasia implies the loss of a
previously existing function. Because in the case of children the

function has never been developed, there is much controversy regarding the usefulness of the application of the term "aphasia" to children and the term "dysphasia" is therefore preferred. In children whose severe language disabilities cannot be explained on the basis of deafness, emotional deprivation, or mental retardation, delayed language and speech development is one of the earliest and more sensitive indicators of a child with organic neurological impairment. Unless these children can be identified and helped at an early age, they inevitably have difficulty in learning school subjects, particularly reading, writing and spelling.

Developmental Dyslexia

The whole concept of specific developmental dyslexia, or as it is sometimes termed, "congenital word blindness", has been the subject of much controversy between neurologists, teachers and educational psychologists. In his book *Reading Disability*, Hermann (1959) describes it as "a specific disorder of function and not merely the chance result of a series of external factors". Children fall behind in reading for various reasons. Many teachers and some educational psychologists hold that reading failure in children can usually be explained by mental subnormality, emotional maladjustment, wrong teaching methods, wrong timing of the introduction to formal reading lessons before the child was "ready" to begin, or by adverse environmental factors. Possibly, the child may be suffering from more than one of these contributory causes. Nevertheless, the concept of specific congenital dyslexia has been retained for some half a century, particularly by medical disciplines.

As early as 1895 an ophthalmologist, Hinshelwood, was writing in medical journals on word blindness and visual memory. In his book on *Congenital Word Blindness* in 1917, he presented his descriptive thesis of this condition. As an ophthalmologist, he had examined the visual acuity of patients who had completely failed to learn to read. He found that their vision was not the cause of their difficulty, but that they had a grave defect in the visual memory centre and that there was a striking contrast between the capacity of the auditory and visual memories. He described in some detail methods that were tried to teach these patients to read by circumventing their defect.

Since then, much has been written both in America and in Europe regarding this specific reading disability. It is characterized by the following:

1. It is not related to peripheral visual defect.
2. It is not related to peripheral auditory defect.
3. It can occur in children of any level of intelligence.
4. It is not related to visuo-spatial disability.
5. It is closely associated with delayed language development.
6. It is a familial or inherited disability.
7. It is characterized by reversals of letters and confusion in the order of letters in words long after the normal child, through the process of maturation, has outgrown these difficulties, so that children with specific developmental dyslexia continue to have difficulty in sequencing and orientation.
8. It is thought by some, e.g. Zangwill (1960) to be associated with undefined cerebral dominance.

Writing of congenital word blindness, Hermann (1959) described it as follows:

> a defective capacity for acquiring at the normal time a proficiency in reading and writing corresponding to average performance; the deficiency is dependent on constitutional factors (heredity), is often accompanied by difficulties with other symbols (numbers, musical notation, etc.), it exists in the absence of intellectual defect or of defects of the sense organs which might retard the normal accomplishment of these skills and in the absence of past or present appreciable inhibitory influences in the internal and external environments.

Danish workers assess the incidence of this condition among school children as 10 per cent, Hallgren (1950). It is difficult to make an assessment in this country, since there is still considerable confusion regarding diagnosis.

Critchley (1964) describes it as "a defect in the visual interpretation of verbal symbols, an aphasia-like state; part of an inherent linguistic defect", and in his Doyne Memorial Lecture (1961) on *Inborn Reading Disorders of Central Origin* he says:

> Within the community of poor readers there exists a specific syndrome wherein the particular difficulty exists in learning the conventional meaning of symbols. Such cases are earmarked by their gravity and their purity. The syndrome is of constitutional and not of environmental origin and is often genetically determined. It is independent of the factor of intelligence and may appear in children of normal I.Q. The difficulty is not due to peripheral visual defects but represents highest level a-symbolia.

Writing in the Seattle Seguin School Collection of Studies of Learning Disorder, Johnson and Myklebust (1965) describe dyslexia as not just a reading disorder, but rather a part of a basic language and learning disability in which the child's main deficit is at the level of symbolization.

Despite the conflicting opinions regarding the reality of a specific reading disability such as Critchley and others describe, it would seem that there are some children who have very severe difficulty in learning to read and that their disability is related to a specific developmental language disorder. These children are slow to speak and also late in comprehending speech, so that this kind of reading disability could be regarded as a disorder of the most highly developed functions of language and language skills.

Although in all the characteristics of the groups of children described above there are learning difficulties due primarily to either congenital factors or early brain injury, no one method of remedial teaching is appropriate for all. Having identified these children, the first essential in planning a suitable treatment programme is in every case a careful diagnostic assessment of the individual child.

CHAPTER 2

Early Learning

As was shown in the previous chapter, comparatively little research has been done on ways of identifying deviant development in pre-school children. In order to identify those children whose level of functioning in certain areas deviates more widely than can be accounted for by slow normal development, it is essential to have in one's mind a clear picture of young children's mental development, in order to judge when a child's levels of ability fall so far outside the norms as to raise the question of the need for further investigation.

Though every child is a unique personality and develops in his own entirely personal way, the various studies concerning the physical, mental, emotional and social development of infants and young children have provided us with some recognizable standards or trends by which a child's individual progress can be judged.

It is not the purpose here to describe these in detail. This has been done very fully by Gesell *et al.* (1940), Illingworth (1960) and more recently, Landreth (1967) as well as many others. The aim here is to give a brief overall picture of the way in which the child's early learning develops to the point when he is ready and equipped to start school and on the basis of this, to suggest pointers to early identification of children with possible disorders of learning.

The problem of early identification of children who are likely to have difficulties when they reach school age is extremely complex. The course of development in infancy and early childhood is determined by the interplay of inherent capacity, maturation and learning, as it is related to the total interaction of physical, mental, social and emotional factors. It is not only physical handicaps, disorders of movement and sensory abnormalities, but also lack of emotional satisfaction that can create delayed and deviant maturation and as a consequence, delayed and disorderly experiences and opportunities for learning. The boundaries of developmental norms of the learning of pre-school children are so wide and difficult to define clearly that it is not easy to be sure that a delay in one area of development is necessarily a pointer to the probability that the child has suffered damage, or has an inherent disability that will create for him the kind of learning difficulties in school that are increasingly thought to arise from cerebral dysfunction.

In this account of the main trends in the development of learning in young children, the same broad chronological stages as are put forward by Piaget will be followed. According to Piaget (1950) the child's intellectual development follows a definite sequence, in which different kinds of thinking follow one another. Although maturation plays a necessary part in the child's development, Piaget emphasizes also the importance of experience, particularly in the child's activities with objects during infancy and early childhood. Piaget describes the major stages of cognitive development as follows:

1. Sensori-motor Period

During this first period, the infant moves from the reflex level of undifferentiation of himself from his surroundings to a coherent organization of sensori-motor actions in relation to his immediate environment. This period involves simple perceptual and motor adjustments to perceived objects, rather than symbolic manipulations of them. Piaget describes the first period as the "sensori-motor" phase lasting up to about 18 months to 2 years of age. To a certain extent, much of the behaviour which Piaget observed during this period has been recorded by the many students of infant behaviour, such as Gesell *et al.* (1940), Buhler

(1945), Bayley (1943), Illingworth (1960) and others. Piaget, however, was always concerned, through study of the child's behaviour, to gain insight into what the behaviour revealed about the way the world appeared to the infant. During this "sensori-motor" period, the child gains knowledge of the world around him through all his senses—sight, hearing, touch, smell, taste. This is the period when the child learns about his world, as Piaget describes it, by "*active* exploration of the environment and continual organisation and reorganisation of sense impressions derived from it".

Piaget (1953) and (1955) traces in revealing detail the way in which the infant's earliest reflexes are modified through the active experimentation of very young children. He describes the first phase of this "sensori-motor" period, that is approximately the first month of life, as the period during which the infant simply exercises the reflexes that are present at birth. From roughly 1 to 4 months, the infant begins to co-ordinate his reflexes and his responses, so that, for example, hand movements are co-ordinated with eye movements and this enables the child to reach out to touch and grasp an object. Similarly, he turns to look towards what he hears. Gradually, throughout this "sensori-motor" period, the infant's use of reflexes is modified through his contact with his environment and he develops adaptive behaviour rather than mere reflexes.

This process of modification comes about by some kind of internalizing of experience, which Piaget describes as "assimilation". The changes which come about in behavioural development as a result of "assimilation" of experience are described by Piaget as "accommodation".

The birth reflexes are the foundation stones on which the child's adaptive behaviour is built and this has some relevance to the disorderly development of the child who is brain-injured from birth.

During this early period of development, the child gradually becomes aware of the permanence of objects, so that his behaviour becomes more purposeful. By the end of this sensori-motor phase,

from about 18 months to 2 years onwards, a normally developing
child shows, in so far as can be judged from his play behaviour,
that he has completed the process of distinguishing between
himself and the objects in his environment. He shows by his actions that he can recognize objects as having a separate existence
from himself, that they are related in space and that they can be
moved by agents other than himself. By this time, if a desired
object is hidden from him, he will actively search for it. He will
drop objects to watch them fall and pull toys to within his reach
with strings, or use a stick to draw the object nearer. Between
18 months and 2 years of age, the child begins to show the capacity
to think about objects that are not immediately observable by
him. He shows some degree of remembering, planning and imagining. His world is no longer bound by what he directly perceives.
He has reached the period of the beginnings of representational
thought.

2. Pre-conceptual Stage

This second phase of mental development—that is from
approximately 2 to 4 years of age—is described by Piaget as the
symbolic and pre-conceptual stage. An understanding of this
period is extremely important for those who are concerned with
early identification of pre-school children who are likely to have
specific learning problems on starting formal school.

The fact that a child can respond to an object without directly
perceiving it implies that he has developed the ability to represent
the object for himself symbolically in some other form. Piaget
holds that this representation takes place for the young child in
the form of a memory image and this he believes to be an important
bridge in the process from sensori-motor to symbolic thinking.
During this developmental period, the use of imagery or "symbolic function" is greatly aided by the acquisition of language. It
is in this period that children indulge in play that is imitative and
symbolical. In his discussion of *Play, Dreams and Imitation in
Childhood* Piaget (1951) suggests that imaginative play at this age

serves a function similar to that of language itself. In describing a series of observational studies of the play of groups of children between ages 2 and 6, Lunzer (1959) writes: "Dramatic play is best regarded as a form of thinking in which the thought is externalised in action because the speech mechanism is as yet insufficiently developed to function unaided". This period of 2–4 years is in the normal child essentially a period of maximum development of the use of language, though in the early stages, a young child can more easily express himself in symbolic play than in words. Piaget makes a distinction between "symbolic play", which he holds occurs after the sensori-motor period of development, and what he terms "practice play" in which during the first eighteen months of life, the infant indulges in repetitive play for the pleasure of exercising a newly learned skill or extending his exploration of his environment, as for example, banging an object on different kinds of surfaces, dropping toys from his pram, rolling a ball, or splashing the water in his bath. In this kind of "practice play", he is learning about objects and his environment by exploration of things that he can actually perceive. In representational or symbolic play, the child uses play to serve a similar function to that served by language at a later stage. Throughout this period, the child remains egocentric in his thinking and reality is frequently distorted.

3. Intuitive thought

During the next period, described by Piaget as the period of intuitive thought, approximately from 4 to 7 years of age, the child develops the ability to form concepts and gradually to construct more complex thoughts and images. When he is able to free his thinking from the domination of his own interests and the influence of what he perceives at a given time, he can come to correct conclusions about concrete aspects of reality, though he is not able to deal with abstractions until a much later age. During this time, the child's language ability increases, so that it gradually becomes for him the main tool of thought.

This is a very much abbreviated account of Piaget's theory of the periods of early development of learning, but it will serve as a background against which early identification of deviantly developing children can be discussed.

Most of Piaget's theory has grown first from careful and accurate observation of his own children, followed later by various experiments, planned to clarify interesting points of theory that have arisen for him through intimate observation of the on-going development of children. Piaget's main interest is in the development of *understanding* in the child. He held that each advance in an infant's sensori-motor behaviour represents an advance in his understanding that is made possible by his experience.

Social Development

Very different kinds of research approaches from that of Piaget are those which study the development of feelings, attachment to persons and objects in the young child. These are of interest and importance in what they reveal of the beginnings of social development in young children.

An interesting series of studies by Schaffer (1958, 1963, 1966 and 1969) form a good example of the way in which he demonstrates the changes in development of some general tendencies in young children, as seen through social attachments and their converse—fear of strangers.

In the course of a well-controlled series of observations of the effect of hospitalization on young children, Schaffer observed two distinct syndromes, depending on the age of the children. The first of these was what has been termed the "deprivation syndrome" and clearly described by Bowlby (1951), Spitz (1945), Goldfarb (1955) and others. This was only observed in children over 7 months of age. Babies under 7 months of age who had been in hospital for periods of 1–2 weeks were found on removal from hospital to be almost unaware of objects and people, even their own mothers. They spent their time gazing round with blank, bewildered expressions. This behaviour, which Schaffer calls the "global syndrome", would seem to have been caused by the prolonged exposure to monotonous and unchanging surroundings where the baby could see little and was seldom nursed or talked to. These babies were described as having become "rigidified and set in the unchanging perceptual environment".

Schaffer points out that the ability to establish attachments to specific individuals first occurs several months later than the capacity to differentiate perceptually between familiar and unfamiliar people, which occurs in the normally developing infant at about 4 months of age. Writing of the child's construction of reality, Piaget (1955) distinguishes between the change after about 6 months of age in the infant's ability to organize his perceptions round permanent objects, which he recognizes as having independent existence in time and space. In the earlier period, an infant begins to apprehend his world in terms of a series of images which can be recognized but which have no substance or permanence. In the early months, the child gains from attention and stimulation, without which he suffers "sensory deprivation", but later, from 6 or 7 months, when he has developed to the stage of recognizing the permanence of objects, he is able not only to recognize certain specific individuals, but to become emotionally attached to them and to seek them in their own right.

Schaffer concludes from this study that the more widely known effects of hospitalization—the "deprivation syndrome"—does not arise until the child has become aware of the permanence of objects apart from himself and that this awareness is developed after the age of 7 months. Until he has reached that stage in his development, there can be no deprivation syndrome because he is not yet aware of a "Mother" as a permanent and separate being, with whom he has formed an attachment and whom he misses when separated from her. The global syndrome is thought by Schaffer to be caused by the differences between the amount of stimulation experienced in the home and hospital environments and is caused by "sensory deprivation". In a further study, Schaffer (1963, 1966) shows that the age at which the infant develops fear of strangers occurs at least a month later than the onset of attachment behaviour, which he places at about 7 or 8 months of age. Perception of strangers and unfamiliarity can only occur when the infant's perceptual experiences in social situations are founded on his ability to distinguish familiar from unfamiliar individuals.

Schaffer shows from his research studies that fear of strangers is a multi-determined event. There is, nevertheless, at its core the experience of discrepancy between the sensory information provided by an unfamiliar individual and a central pattern corresponding to the familiar person.

In a later study, Schaffer and Parry (1969) show that there is a period of development extending to some point in the second half-year of an infant's life before recognition occurs based on previous memory of familiar and unfamiliar objects and the ability to distinguish actively between them. To quote, "At 12 months the infant not only perceives but also acts selectively in relation to the familiarity–unfamiliarity dimension and a new kind of integration can thus be seen to have taken place. . . . The achievement of such integration may be regarded as a fundamental step in the infant's construction of his environment".

The work of Schaffer provides an interesting example of the way in which a study started from a quite different premise throws confirmatory light on the progress of the gradual development of the infant's recognition of himself as separate from the people and objects that form his environment.

Development of Visual Perception

Before leaving this discussion of learning in pre-school children, some reference must be made to Vernon's (1962, 1965) work on the development of visual perception. Vernon holds that a study of the development of the child's perceptual capacities is essential to an understanding of the way in which the child establishes and maintains contacts with the world around him. In her detailed account of the way in which the child learns to perceive the world around him, she shows how the child's perceptual development starts from early infancy, that is, Piaget's substage of "reflex schemata", when the infant begins with a vague awareness of sensory patterns which have little meaning for him. Gradually, by maturing in the ability to co-ordinate what began as independent movements, the infant can associate visual and auditory sensations with the same object and can use his vision to direct his hands towards a perceived object in order to grasp it. By this kind of exploration, the child gradually begins to have some understanding of the nature of solid objects, of shapes and sizes, and he learns to relate two-dimensional outlines to the three-dimensional objects which they represent. Although he can discriminate between shapes at an early age, he cannot reproduce them accurately until much later.

This gradual process of development of spatial and shape perception is aptly summarized by Vernon (1965):

> The child must learn how to view a complex field, directing his attention appropriately and extracting its essential and significant features until he is able not only to perceive readily those parts which are interesting and important to him but also to compare and assess the sizes and distance of objects in surrounding space. He must also acquire the capacity to perceive and understand significant changes in the environment while ignoring those that are relatively unimportant, such as changes of shape in the outlines of objects rotated into various positions. In doing this he is assisted firstly by his manipulation of objects, when he grasps, fingers and handles them and moves them about in space; and later by reasoning about them, their functions and inter-relationships in words.

To progress satisfactorily in school learning, the child needs intact sensory equipment with which to gain experience of the world around him; he needs to develop motor skills and the use of language and, most important, he needs the capacity to integrate all these in his functioning. Only in this way can he develop for himself a stable and predictable perceptual world.

Language Development

Language is a very important aspect of mental growth, particularly during the pre-school years. Since we are concerned here with ways of recognizing children for whom the course of development is so deviant that it points to the possibility that the child should have special help, we need to have an understanding of the development in young children of the use of language symbols and its relevance to later learning disorders. Language is the symbolization of thought. It is a system of symbols used to represent objects, ideas and feelings. Before a child uses the spoken word, he first must have meaningful experience. Writing of the developmental sequence in the acquisition of language by the normal child, in his study of the psychology of deafness, Myklebust (1964) says:

> The child does not first learn words and then the meaning; meaningfulness and experience precede the acquisition of words to symbolise experience. The relating of experience and symbol is the basis of *inner language*. As this process develops the child can think in words, he can use mental trial and error, he can group and classify his experiences.

Myklebust suggests that the child needs a period of from 6 to 9 months, during which time he is beginning to develop inner language, before he can begin to comprehend the spoken word. From roughly the age of 9 to 12 months, the child begins to comprehend. Myklebust describes this process as that of "internalizing the word in a rudimentary way". At first, he can only do this with words which symbolize his own basic experiences, but this process of relating sound which he hears to his known experience is the beginning of "receptive language". After about the age of 12 months, during which both inner and receptive language are developed, the child begins to use the spoken word —expressive language. Although developmentally the sequence is for inner language to be acquired first, receptive language next, followed in the period from 12 months to 2 years with expressive language, the course of development is not clear-cut. Throughout all this period, the later stages of development influence and enhance the skills acquired previously, though receptive language only begins to develop after a foundation of inner language has been laid and expressive language can only be accomplished after comprehension has been established. The child begins to speak after he has begun to comprehend.

An understanding of the course of the development of spoken

language during the period of early childhood, the 2–4 years' period or Piaget's "pre-conceptual stage", is of particular relevance in the study of normal development in the pre-school years.

Inner Language

Sheridan (1964) describes inner language as a personal store of concepts-in-code, this has emotional as well as intellectual components, which differ for every individual. She holds that "the possession of inner language depends on the child's ability to organize the percepts derived from his multi-sensorial experiences into meaningful concepts" and she continues:

> It is difficult to know how and precisely when the transition from naming to the use of true symbolic language occurs, but from personal observations made in day nurseries and hospital units for children with disorders of communication, I have reached the conclusion that the outward sign that a child has come into possession of an "inner language" is his first use of make-believe in play. Make-believe in play, in which the child reflects his everyday experiences, emotional reactions and general understanding, is an activity unique to human young. It is evidence that the child can not only evoke symbols from his inner language repository at will, but that he can manipulate them to create something new and personal to himself. . . . The so-called "non-communicating" child, whether his language disability is due to developmental anomaly, to brain injury or to psychosis, does not seem to possess similar capacity to "make sense" of his world, that is to integrate his physical, mental and emotional experiences. He does not play at "let's pretend". His inability to express his thoughts and feelings in any symbolic form appears to be secondary to his developmental lack, or subsequent loss of an "inner language".

Growth of Understanding

The pre-conceptual period, roughly from 18 months to 4 years, is the period during which the child's growth of understanding occurs by means first of symbolic play, through which he deals with his problems by imitation or representation of objects or actions taken out of their original context. Gradually during this stage, he is developing the use of verbal symbols and as he nears

4 years of age he proceeds from the stage of symbolic play to intuitive thought, which is aided greatly by his use of language. Speech is becoming for him a regulator of his activities and a tool of thought.

Deviations from Normal Development

Even though there are considerable individual differences among children in their *rate* of development, wide discrepancies in the growth of abilities in the individual child are unusual and call for further investigation. It is interesting that in her studies of severely defective children, Woodward (1959 and 1962) shows how the stage identified by Piaget during the sensori-motor period of development of normal children up to 18 months can be traced in these severely defective children, though they occur at a much older chronological age. This, in Woodward's view, confirms the sequence of stages delineated by Piaget for normal children. Some mildly brain-damaged children show marked unevenness in their development. For example, even in the early "sensori-motor" phase, it would seem that there is evidence in some infants of an impairment of the capacity for normal perceptual development. This is seen in a study carried out under the direction of Honzik (1960) and Honzik *et al.* (1965). This was designed to compare the pattern of success and failure on the Bayley Infant Mental and Motor Scales of infants suspected of neurological deficits, with that of normal infants. The babies were tested at 8 months of age, using this infant test. The main purpose of the study was to evaluate the discriminatory power of the tests and not primarily to study the relation of specific neurological difficulties to test performance. Nevertheless, Honzik found that there were some test items passed by the "suspect" babies more frequently than the control group of "normal" infants. The "suspect" babies passed a larger proportion of the verbal and social items, while the "normal" infants passed more items involving alert attentiveness and adaptive response to the test materials.

In her presentation of Paul, a spastic left hemiplegic, Meyer Taylor (1959) describes his behaviour at 15 months as follows:

Paul is retarded in motor development and limited in his ability to get around and use his hands. His contact with the world of objects remains superficial. He shows little initiative and enterprise because most stimuli remain undifferentiated and unspecific for him and leave no prolonged imprint. His undifferentiated and scantily adapted responses make him socially a friendly baby who smiles at everybody and everything. His invariably good-natured attitude masks a lack of discrimination of the finer shadings and moods which cause a normal baby to be shy and over-sensitive to new impressions.

The behaviour pattern she described from her very wide experience as characteristic of the hemiplegic children she has known, is very similar to the behavioural pattern that emerges from the examination of the responses in the Bayley tests in Honzik's studies. Even as early as 8 months, we see in the "suspect" babies a differential response to their world, which would seem to be due to differences in visuo-motor perceptual ability.

One of the striking characteristics of many brain-damaged children who have visuo-spatial disability is the extent to which their language development remains unrelated to the development of their visuo-perceptual abilities. Writing of cerebral palsied children, Denhoff and Robinault (1960) suggest that many of them are damaged in their "central co-ordinating equipment". Failure in integration appears to be at the core also of the problem of many non-physically handicapped children who have special learning difficulties at school and who show big discrepancies between verbal and performance tests, such as the Wechsler Scales for Pre-school and School Age Children. Studies by Bortner and Birch (1962), Birch and Lefford (1963) and Birch and Belmont (1965) show that children with cerebral palsy are significantly defective in their ability to integrate information derived from the auditory, visual and kinaesthetic sense modalities with one another. They suggest that disturbed inter-sensory patterning not only underlies certain of the perceptual and visuo-motor disturbances found in some cerebral palsied children, but also that poor inter-sensory integration affects the development of behaviour.

This leaves us with the problem of the means by which children who are likely to have difficulties in school arising from disorderly development can be identified in pre-school years and, if identified, how they can be helped before starting formal learning. It is with this problem that the research study described in detail in the next chapter is concerned.

CHAPTER 3

A Research Study into the Early Identification of Pre-school Children likely to have Specific Learning Disorders

CHILDREN who are mentally subnormal in a global sense show an overall retardation in all areas of development and can be early recognized and helped. Less easily recognizable at a pre-school age are those children of normal intelligence who, in consequence of neurodevelopmental learning disorders, suffer from an unevenness in different areas of performance, so serious as to be likely to lead to "specific" learning difficulties in the future. In this context, "specific" means a defect of functioning in a particular area, compared with the child's overall level of performance, be it high, average or low.

These children are difficult to identify because normal children rarely perform evenly throughout the whole range of their abilities. This is particularly true of young pre-school children, who may frequently appear to stand still in one area of development while racing ahead in another. It may therefore be difficult to distinguish a child with neurodevelopmental learning disorders from one who, for example, while developing motor skills at a sudden rapid rate, may almost come to a halt in his use of language for the time being. This is not due in any sense to a defect of functioning, but is purely a temporary phase, while all his energies are absorbed in gaining skill in running, jumping, balancing and climbing.

The research study described below was undertaken to examine the possibility of identifying by means of tests, observations of behaviour and rating scales, those children whose development was so uneven that there was a very real possibility that they might run into difficulties on starting formal schooling.

Before starting the research study proper, an exploratory study was made of aspects of perceptual development in a group of 3- and 4-year-old children, attending the Tavistock Clinic nursery school in London. The purpose of this exploratory study was to examine the value of various tests of pre-school children and to compile a battery of tests which would be practical in use and useful as discriminators in the research study proper.

This exploratory period threw into relief some of the difficulties. The first was the very wide range of levels of development in this group of "normal" children. The whole pattern of development in these young children appeared to be greatly complicated by the effects of emotional satisfactions and of maturation of the early development of the child.

While it is comparatively easy to recognize and assess the extent of disability in a school child of, say, eight or nine years and to measure its severity in comparison with a normally developing 8- or 9-year-old, the assessment of such disability in children of pre-school years is much more problematic. Unless the disorders due to cerebral dysfunction are very severe, it is very difficult indeed to distinguish children suffering these disorders from slow normal development in young children.

Writing of visuo-spatial handicap in children with cerebral palsy, Ram (1962), a teacher very experienced in this field, says, "It is tempting to try to identify all the children with visuo-spatial difficulty in the pre-school years but normal development rates vary so much from child to child that at this early age it is impossible to be sure that you are dealing with a specific disability". She was discussing here children with cerebral palsy attending a school for cerebral palsied children. She knew these children well and saw them regularly each day. To identify specific visuo-spatial difficulties in children whose damage is much less, inevitably presents an even greater problem.

For purposes of the research study, it was essential to use suitable tests standardized on young children. This was not easy, since there was comparatively little published work on young children in this field of study. However, the following seemed worthy of further consideration.

In order to study the relationships of perinatal anoxia to intelligence and neurological deviations in the pre-school child, Graham *et al.* (1960, 1962 and 1963) constructed a psychological test battery, suitable for ages ranging from 3 to $5\frac{1}{2}$ years, which is designed to tap those functions thought to be most sensitive to damage to the central nervous system. Their tests are designed to measure aspects of perceptual-motor ability, conceptual ability and personality characteristics. For their research purposes, they finally used the following battery of tests:

1. *Vocabulary scale*. This scale was composed of verbal sub-tests from the 1937 Stanford-Binet Intelligence Scale. It included picture vocabulary and definitions tests from forms L and M and the word vocabulary test from form L. These items were administered and scored according to instructions in the Binet manual (Terman and Merrill, 1937). Where necessary to establish a basal vocabulary age, a number of words and combinations-of-words items from the Cattell (1940) Infant Intelligence Scale were also included.

2. *Concepts or block-sort test*. This test was designed and standardized for the purpose by Ernhart and Graham. It is a test of ability to match or group blocks according to colour, size and form. It is designed to tap the ability to group according to concepts at a simpler level than those employed by Goldstein and Sheerer (1941).

3. *Perceptual-motor tests*. These included a test of *copying forms*, designed and standardized for use with young children, by Graham *et al.* (1960).

Motor-co-ordination test. In this, the child is required to draw lines between three concentric figures, a circle, a square and a triangle, without crossing the boundaries of any figure. There was also a group of tests, designated the perceptual-motor battery, which consisted of the following sub-tests:

(i) *Figure-ground test*. In this, the child was asked to identify the thirty-five objects from the Binet Picture Vocabulary, forms L and M, when these were reproduced on distracting backgrounds.

(ii) *Tactual-localization sub-test*. This is an adaptation of Bender's Face–Hand test (Fink and Bender, 1953).

(iii) *Mark-the-cars sub-test*, in which the child was asked to place a mark on each of the drawings of cars (ten in all) distributed amongst twenty drawings of other objects.

(iv) *Peripheral-distraction sub-test*. In this test, a sheet of white paper represented a table, in the centre of which the child was asked to place a cardboard vase of flowers. Peripheral distractors, a toy glass and a plate were varied in position in the four trials that were given. The score was based on the measure of deviation towards or away from the distractors, in the centring position of the vase.

During the testing of the child, the parent was required to sort 209 cards, each of which described a kind of behaviour. The parent was asked to sort these as being like, unlike or doubtfully like his child.

The examiners also rated the children for eight traits. Four of these—hyperactivity, demandingness, distractibility, and impulsivity—were chosen as "brain-injury" ratings and four others—infantilism, negativism, fearfulness and compulsivity—were considered to be "maladjustment" ratings.

All these, together also with other tests such as the Frostig Developmental Test of Visual Perception by Frostig *et al.* (1961) and also measures of emotional adjustment using projective techniques, such as Anthony and Bene's Family Relations Test (1957) and Rorschach applied to work with children were experimented with in the pilot study year at the Tavistock Nursery School.*

This was a valuable experimental period, from which many useful factors emerged. It was on the basis of information gained during this experimental period that the research plan proper was planned. The final research plan was, therefore, strongly dictated by what was learnt from the pilot study.

Factors Emerging from the Pilot Study

(I) Perhaps the most striking factor that emerged from this study of 3- and 4-year-olds, attending a nursery school for children of comfortably off middle-class, mainly professional parents, was the very wide variation in levels of development among the children. Since it has not been possible to obtain reliable information on the birth histories of all the children attending the nursery, this experimental study emphasized the importance of basing the research on a much more rigorous selection of cases.

(II) On the basis of the varying findings gathered from this sample study and with the limited number of personnel who could devote time to it, it seemed clear that the most useful kind of study would be an intensive one of a small sample of children, taken from a stable and homogeneous population.

(III) In view of the wide differences observed in the relations with the children and the quality of testing, even although the students who took part in giving the tests were all senior students nearing the end of their training, it was decided that the testing in the research study proper should be carried out as far as possible by one person only.

* I am indebted to Dr. John Bowlby for giving facilities for the study to be carried out and to Mrs. Osborne and her students who co-operated so fully: also to Miss Harrison, the nursery school teacher, who not only cheerfully tolerated all the interruptions that such a study as this inevitably involves, but actively contributed to it by her knowledge of the children and her lively interest in the work; finally to the parents, who allowed their children to take part and to the children themselves from whom we learnt so much.

(IV) Selection of a suitable test battery. Since the children selected for the research proper would attend a hospital clinic, it was important to use a battery of tests that it would be possible to carry out during one, or at most two visits. The tests must have an inherent appeal and hold the interest of a normal pre-school child. Also, they must not be too time-consuming, must have a realistic range of difficulty, must be scorable objectively and yield scores amenable to statistical analysis. It was clear that the use of projective techniques could not have a place in the study.

Although the study had originally been stimulated by the need to understand more about the development of perceptual and visuo-spatial ability in young children, observation of the children in the nursery class very quickly demonstrated the importance of language development throughout these pre-school years.

The kind of personality and behavioural assessment used in the Graham study was found to be quite outside the scope of this study. American parents are early familiarized with these kinds of rating scale or inventory, which are commonly used in clinics for children throughout the States but it is quite outside the experience of most English mothers, particularly working-class parents.

Bearing in mind these findings, therefore, the following battery of tests and procedure was chosen.

1. *Copy-forms Test*

This test was standardized by Graham *et al.* (1963). It consists of eighteen forms, printed on 5 in. by 8 in. cards, with one form to a card. The cards are presented one at a time, in the order and position shown in Fig. 1—and the child is asked to copy what is on the card, on a separate paper for each form.

This test has been carefully analysed for scoring of the various abilities that enter into successful achievements. The test is scored for reproducing certain general features of the design—

form as opposed to scribbling, linearity or curvilinearity, the open–closed appearance and the correct number of parts. The main emphasis of the scoring system, however, is on the accurate reproduction of four characteristics, namely the general configuration, orientation on the background, size relationships of parts and intersections.

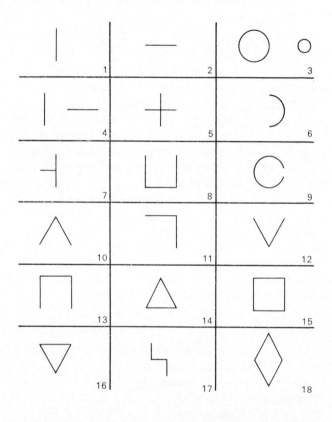

FIG. 1. Graham's Copy Forms Test. (Development in Pre-School Children of the Ability to Copy Forms, Frances K. Graham, Phyllis W. Berman and Claire B. Ernhart, *Child Development*, **31,** 339–359 (1966), The Society for Research in Child Development.)

2. *Concepts or Block Sort Test*

This test also was standardized and was made available for my use by Drs. Graham and Ernhart.

The test consists of twenty-six blocks in various combinations of three colours, white, red and blue, three forms, circle, square and equilateral triangle, and three sizes, small, medium and large. There are also three formboards, each of which has three recesses, into which blocks can be placed. The first board is divided into three equal sections, painted respectively red, white and blue. Each section contains a large circular recess. The other two formboards are painted white. One has recesses for a large, medium and small circle. The other has recesses for the three large forms—triangle, circle and square. The materials vary with respect to three concepts—colour, size and form. There are four difficulty levels. Level I requires placing blocks in the formboards, level II involves matching and levels III and IV require sorting.

The illustrations in Plate 1 shows a normal 4-year-old girl (one of the controls) doing test items from level IV. Level IV is the most difficult part of the test. The task is to sort nine blocks, which vary in two ways, into groups of blocks that are alike. Plate 1a, b and c, shows her doing the test at level IVa, the first trial on which colour and size vary, while form is held constant. These she very quickly sorted for colour. The most difficult level, IVc, in which size and form are varied while colour is held constant, is illustrated in Plate 2a–f. She found this very much more difficult and at first put them all in one pile, saying they were all the same because they were all white. Encouraged to try again, she managed it, making thoughtful observations as she accomplished the task, ending in a note of triumph.

This test has been used at the four-year psychological examination of the children in the American Collaborative Study of Cerebral Palsy, Mental Retardation and other neurological and sensory disorders of infancy and childhood. For use in this project, the Perinatal Research Branch of the National Institute of Neurological Disease and Blindness has published a very useful manual (1963) of instruction.

3. *Self-concept*

In order to assess the child's self-concept, he was asked to draw a picture of himself. This was scored according to Harris' (1963) revision of the Goodenough Drawing of a Man Scale.

4. *Tactual-Localization Test*

The child was also given Graham's adaptation of Bender's Face–Hand test, described by Fink and Bender (1953). This is a tactual-localization test in which objects in the environment, a part of the child's body, or two parts simultaneously are touched by the examiner. The child is asked to identify the object or body part which has been touched. If the child cannot manage to do this with his eyes closed, or will not co-operate with eyes closed, the test is administered with the child's eyes open. Variations in the part and side of the body stimulated, affect the difficulty of the test items. While pointing is the response desired, verbal responses or visual fixation are credited, in so far as is possible. Items are arranged in nine difficulty levels and it is assumed that a child passing at one level will pass all easier items, and failing at one level will fail all the more difficult items. There is only one test situation for each difficulty level, but two to five trials are given.

The tactual-localization form is arranged as in Table 1.

In the Tavistock experimental study, an attempt was made to assess figure–ground discrimination by comparing the number of pictures correctly identified in the Binet Picture Vocabulary scale with those identified when presented on distracting backgrounds.

The children had so little difficulty with this test that it was decided not to use it. Those who could recognize two-dimensional pictures could also recognize them even when presented against distracting backgrounds. Similarly, the mark-the-car test was abandoned because the children found it too easy.

5. *A Test of Verbal Ability*

It had seemed during the pilot study that the verbal items on the Stanford–Binet would provide an adequate assessment of verbal ability in these children but, although the research project was

(a)

(b)

(c)

PLATE 1. Graham's Concepts or Block Sort Test. Level IVa.

(a)

(b)

(c)

PLATE 2. Graham's Concepts or Block Sort Test. Level IVc.

(d)

(e)

(f)

PLATE 2. (continued)

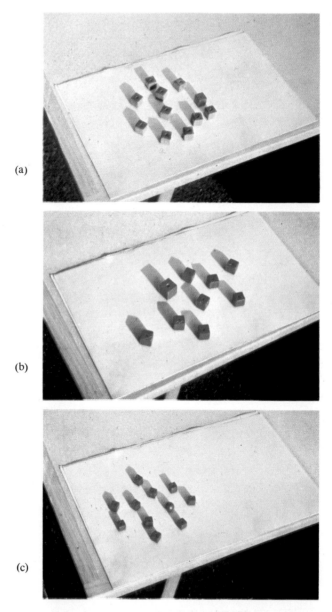

PLATE 3. Exercises for figure-ground work book: simple discriminations on "Find the Stranger".

TABLE 1. TACTUAL LOCALIZATION (REVISED 9.12.56)

Name:
Date:

Enter + or − under the appropriate trial. Incorrect responses should be described in space following stimulus. When response is to only one of two stimuli, circle the one identified.

Item	Trials				
	1	2	3	4	5
A 1. Points to objects incorrectly (eyes open)					
2. Points to objects correctly (eyes open)					
B 3. Discriminates self from object (eyes open)	Left hand	Right shoulder	Left cheek	Right hand	Left shoulder
4. Part or side correct (eyes open)					
5. Part and side correct (eyes open)					
C 6. Part and side correct (eyes closed)	Right cheek	Left shoulder	Right hand	Left hand	Right shoulder
D 7. Same part—opposite sides. Both correct (eyes closed)	Right cheek–Left cheek	Right hand–left hand	Right shoulder–left shoulder	Right cheek–left cheek	Right hand–left hand
E 8. Different part—same side. Both correct (eyes closed)	Right shoulder–right cheek	Left hand–left cheek	Right hand–right shoulder	Left shoulder–left cheek	Right hand–right cheek
F 9. Different part—different side Both correct (eyes closed)	Left hand–right cheek	Right shoulder–left cheek	Left hand–right shoulder	Right hand–left cheek	Left shoulder–right cheek

originally envisaged as being a study of perceptual development of pre-school children, observations during the pilot study at the Tavistock Nursery School quickly emphasized the major importance of language development and its inextricable influence on

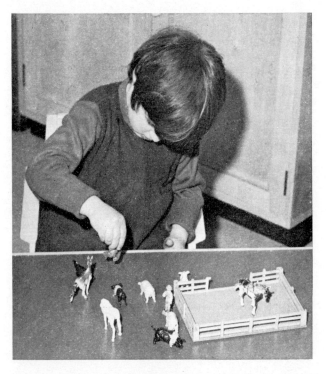

FIG. 2. Test of verbal comprehension: (a) "Put the brown hen beside the black hen".

development in all spheres of learning. For these reasons, it seemed essential to use a more detailed measure of development of verbal ability. I am indebted to Dr. Joan Reynell for allowing me to use her developmental language scales, although then still in their experimental stage. They proved to be of great value. These scales are specifically designed for the separate assessment of receptive and expressive aspects of language. There are three separate scales:

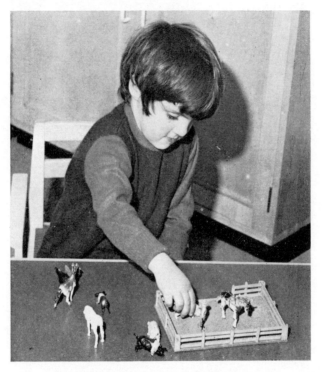

FIG. 2 (b) "Put one of the pigs behind the man".

Verbal comprehension is assessed by use of objects and toys. Verbal comprehension A requires no speech, but does require some hand function. Verbal comprehension B is an adaptation of scale A, for use with severely handicapped children who have neither speech nor hand function. It starts with tasks to demonstrate simple understanding.

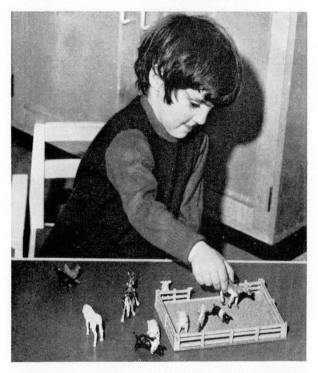

FIG. 2 (c) "Make one of the horses walk through the gateway".

Where is the   1. ball?
                      2. brick?
                      3. brush?
                      4. cup?
                      5. doll?
                      6. car?
                      7. sock?
                      8. spoon?

In this section, except for the toy car, which every child knows well, real objects and no miniature toys are used, because this taps the pre-symbolic stage of development.

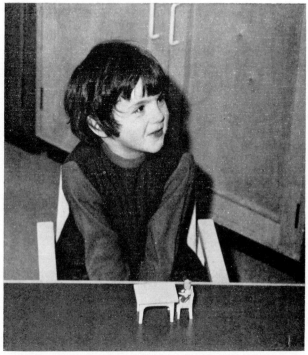

FIG. 2 (d) "This little boy has spilt his dinner. What must he do?"

It then progresses to more difficult levels of understanding from, for example, showing a toy bed, a toy car, etc.

Which one do we   1. sleep in?
                  2. go for a ride in?

to instructions which demand understanding of the required task at progressively more complicated levels:

Example,   "Put the doll on the chair."

                "Put the car in the box."

                "Put the brown hen beside the black hen."

                "Put one of the pigs behind the man."

                "Make one of the horses walk through the gate-way."

Figures 2a, b and c illustrate these.

By not requiring speech for the verbal comprehension scales, verbal comprehension can be assessed completely separately from expressive language. This is a useful distinction for purposes of assessing the language development of the young child. The test has also been constructed with problems of testing severely handicapped children in mind.

For the most difficult level, the test situations, while still presented with toy objects, require some kind of judgement of the situation. Even here, the response need not be made through speech but can be clearly given by demonstration. An example of this is shown in Fig. 2d "This little boy has spilt his dinner. What must he do?"

The expressive language scale is divided into three sections, which may be scored separately or as a whole. They are: (a) language structure, (b) vocabulary, (c) content. Language structure is scored through a carefully designed analysis of the child's use of language. The vocabulary test has three grades of difficulty; the first presents objects for naming and definition, the second a series of pictures and the third requires definition of meaning of words.

The third section, "content", is assessed by the presentation of a series of pictures which the child is required to "look at" and "tell about".

The two scales, verbal comprehension and expressive language, are scored in terms of an equivalent age-level and a standard score for each raw score obtained. The mean of the reliability figures is given for each of the age-groups in the experimental version of the scales, as follows:

Split-half reliability with Spearman correction:

	1–2 years	$2\frac{1}{2}$–$3\frac{1}{2}$ years	4–5 years
Expressive language	0·93	0·85	0·84
Verbal comprehension (A)	0·81	0·90	0·78

Rating Scales

The children were rated at the end of the test interview, and before the examiner or observer who took part in the rating knew to which category the child belonged, for three areas of behaviour which have been thought to be characteristic of the neurologically damaged child, namely:

1. The child's capacity for concentration on a given task.
2. The child's independence.
3. His readiness and ability to co-operate in a task.

A fourth rating scale was used in an attempt to assess the quality of the mother's acceptance of the child. This assessment was much more difficult to make simply on the basis of observations during the test. Mothers from social class V, in their eagerness that the child should do well, were apt to make rather foolish threats, such as "If you don't do what the lady says, I shall go and leave you here"—and the general handling of the child was very different indeed from that of mother in social class I. It was felt, therefore, that a rating of this depth and feeling could not be reliably made on such slender evidence as could be gained in the period of the test interview. After some experimentation, therefore, it was decided not to use it. The ratings were made on a ten point scale, the score ten being the highest score, as for example in 1, capacity for concentration, the score ten is given for the child who showed greatest powers of concentration throughout the whole test period.

Research Design

The purpose of this study was to investigate the possibilities of identification of factors pointing to early recognition of pre-school children who are likely to have specific learning difficulties in certain areas of learning, on starting formal schooling. Using the battery of tests and the rating scales described above, 23 boys and 21 girls, aged 3–4 years, (44 cases) who had been noted at birth as having minor neurological dysfunction were compared with 29 boys and 34 girls (63 controls) who were normal in development.

The children used as controls for this study were quite rigorously chosen. They were all children whom the paediatrician choosing them had known from birth. The criterion for selection was that they had not only a clear birth history, but that the mother had had also normal early, middle and late pregnancy (no threatened miscarriage, no version), normal labour; the baby should have near-normal birth weight, normal neonatal history (no difficulty in starting breathing or crying, no difficulty in sucking or swallowing, no excessive irritability, twitchings or fits, no jaundice before the third or after the eighth day). I am indebted to Dr. R. MacKeith, Consultant Paediatrician at Guy's Hospital, London, for this criterion.

The study was based mainly in Guy's Hospital, but also in St. Luke's Hospital, Guildford, where most of the 4-year-old controls were seen in co-operation with Dr. Stephen Macoun, Consultant Paediatrician to the hospital. Records of the birth of all the children who were reaching four years of age were studied and letters were sent to parents of all the children whose birth histories satisfied Dr. MacKeith's criterion. The purpose of the study was explained to the parents and they were asked if they would be willing to participate.

The children of the parents who agreed to take part had a paediatric vetting and were tested for vision and hearing, just before 4 years of age. Children who had any serious physical defect, as for example, a boy with a very severe squint, were not included in the group finally chosen.

Because the children studied were children whose parents were interested enough to co-operate, the sample is inevitably a biased one. The area served by St. Luke's Hospital, Guildford, is a widespread rural one and journeys to and from the hospital by rather infrequent buses are often difficult. The result was that only the more interested parents co-operated. This is true also of the parents of the children seen in Guy's Hospital. The area round that hospital samples a very different kind of population, whose problems in co-operating in this sort of research, although equally real, are by no means the same. By basing the study on two such dissimilar areas the total sample was made more representative, as will be shown.

The remainder of the 4-year-old controls and all the 3-year-old controls were selected and seen at Guy's Hospital, using the same procedure as had been used at Guildford. All the 3- and 4-year-old cases were selected by Dr. Neil O'Doherty at Guy's Hospital, London.

His method of selection of cases is described by him as follows:

As part of a routine nursery service, the children were all assessed neurologically in the newborn period when the Obstetric Resident sought paediatric advice because there had been significant family history, a high perinatal risk, or some clinical abnormality had been seen. An effort was made to have the child in a good state of arousal by examining him shortly before a feed was due, as far as circumstances allowed, the child was seen on the sixth day.

Approximately twenty items relating to posture, tone and primitive reflexes were tested and abnormalities were classified as apathy, hyperexcitability and/or hemisymdromes [Prechtl and Beintema 1964; O'Doherty, 1963]. Because different test items were favoured by extremes in the baby's state of arousal, it was not uncommon for a normal child's performance to warrant one or two comments, but for the most part significant minor neurological dysfunction could be diagnosed with confidence especially where hemisymdromes were defined. A few children had transient neurological dysfunction of serious degree which required special treatment, e.g. convulsions, or kept them in hospital, e.g. inability to feed.

Over the course of three years, out of a total nursery population of about 3,000, there were 130 children diagnosed as having significant major or minor neurological dysfunction in the newborn period. There were also 70 control children who were examined at the obstetrician's request and recorded as neurologically intact.

The 44 children from the 130 diagnosed as showing minor neurological dysfunction were taken into this study as they reached their third or fourth birthday.

Hand Dominance

Among the cases, six children were definitely left-handed and eight had not developed a clear hand dominance. There was only one left-handed child among the controls and two with no clear hand dominance.

Rating Scales

The meaning of the ratings was very fully discussed by the examiner and her research assistant who took part in the rating, as well as with other colleagues interested in the work, before the final study began.

The children were rated on a ten-point scale for the three areas of behaviour described above. It was stressed that ratings should be based on the *observed* behaviour of the child during the testing session. Judgements, therefore, were made as factual as possible and were based on what was thought to be significant in the children's behaviour, in relation to their attitudes to the test and their behaviour during it. The rating was carried out immediately at the end of each child's test interview, without any knowledge on the part of the examiner as to whether the child was a case or a control. The research assistant also did part-time nursing in the hospital and during the relevant time had known four of the cases who had been back into hospital; one of these had started at $2\frac{1}{2}$ years to have epileptic fits and had intermittently returned to the hospital as an in-patient. Apart from these four children, neither the examiner nor the research assistant knew at the time of the test interview to which category the child belonged.

As a general guide, it was decided that a child should be rated 10 for concentration if he had completed each separate task with a short break between each and was not distracted from the task by the entrance of a stranger during the test. The lowest rating, 1, was given to a child who could not concentrate on any of the tests and was "untestable". The mid-point of the scale 5 was given when a child interrupted most of the test items but when his query was satisfied, he was able to take up the test from where he stopped and complete it.

In the "independence" scale, the top rating of 10 was given where, after the mother and child had been received in the waiting room, the child came happily and fearlessly with the examiner and was able to go through the whole test procedure without wanting to go back to mother or asking where she was. Rating 1 was given when the child would only come to the clinic room, clinging to mother, sat on mother's knee and refused to speak or touch any of the toy or test material without reassurance from mother. The mid-point rating of 5 was given when the child refused to be separated from mother but carried out the test normally if the mother remained in sight in the room, but was not drawn into the test situation.

Co-operation in the test was rated 10 when the child was eager to please and attempted all that he was asked to do. The rating 1 was given if he refused to try anything that was asked of him— neither touched the toys nor spoke in answer to any question and refused to "draw". This needs to be distinguished from fear and shyness in a strange situation which, when overcome, releases normal co-operation. The mid-point 5 was judged to be when a child was "selectively" co-operative, but complied with other tasks without real effort and interest.

Findings

Table 2 shows the level of agreement on the rating scales.

The two raters agreed overall within one point on 89·47 per cent of the observations.

TABLE 2. AGREEMENT ON RATING SCALES
(number of pairs of observations = 428)

	Controls	Cases	All	%
Complete agreement	145	99	244	57·00
Within one point	75	64	139	32·47
Within two points	31	13	44	10·30
Three point disagreement	1	0	1	—
	252	176	428	—

Out of 428 observations, there was only one instance where the examiner and the research assistant disagreed on ratings by more than two points on the scale.

In Table 3, which shows the intercorrelations between the main variables, the measures can be seen to correlate highly with each other. This indicates that the tests are to some extent measuring something in common, which would probably be general ability. The positive correlations with age show that there is a strong developmental component in all these items. This would be expected.

Table 4 shows the means, standard deviations and the difference between means on psychological tests and rating scales for the two groups. The results of tests of self-concept are dealt with separately.

The findings presented in Table 4 show a significantly poorer score on all the tests and on the ratings of the cases than of the controls. It is interesting that the verbal scales and behaviour ratings differentiate between the two groups even more strongly than do the form copying and the block design tests. Although the language difference may, in part, be due to the poorer environmental background than that of the controls (Table 5) the difference is so great that this is unlikely to be a complete explanation. It can reasonably be concluded that the cases have poorer language development than the controls.

TABLE 3. INTERCORRELATIONS OF VARIABLES

(63 controls)

	Age 44·14	Verbal Comprehension	Verbal Language	Form Copying	Block Design	Dependency	Concentration	Co-operation
1. Mean Age in mths.	44·14							
2. Verbal comprehension	0·588	—						
3. Verbal language	0·617	0·718	—					
4. Form copying	0·797	0·637	0·725	—				
5. Block design	0·559	0·535	0·631	0·644	—			
6. Dependency	0·558	0·719	0·761	0·558	0·559	—		
7. Concentration	0·508	0·714	0·761	0·643	0·669	0·767	—	
8. Co-operation	0·410	0·635	0·633	0·574	0·524	0·700	0·825	—

With $N = 63$, $r = 0·245$ is significant at $P = 0·05$.

$r = 0·325$ is significant at $P = 0·01$.

$r = 0·405$ is significant at $P = 0·001$.

(44 cases)

	Age 42·95	Verbal	Verbal	Form	Block	Depen-dency	Concentra-tion	Co-operation
1. Mean Age in months	42·95							
2. Verbal comprehension	0·483	—						
3. Verbal language	0·603	0·902	—					
4. Form copying	0·883	0·550	0·617	—				
5. Block design	0·680	0·789	0·825	0·631	—			
6. Dependency	0·666	0·775	0·828	0·674	0·699	—		
7. Concentration	0·601	0·805	0·836	0·599	0·670	0·793	—	
8. Co-operation	0·565	0·861	0·879	0·544	0·730	0·765	0·939	—

With $N = 44$, $r = 0·280$ is significant at $P = 0·05$.
$r = 0·370$ is significant at $P = 0·01$.
$r = 0·460$ is significant at $P = 0·001$.

TABLE 4. MEANS, STANDARD DEVIATIONS AND SIGNIFICANCE OF
DIFFERENCE BETWEEN MEANS ON PSYCHOLOGICAL TESTS AND RATING SCALES

Variable	63 Controls		44 Cases		Difference between means	Critical ratio	Probability
	Mean	S.D.	Mean	S.D.			
Age in months	44·14	6·96	42·95	7·84	1·19	0·81	N.S.
Verbal comprehension	42·73	7·81	34·09	13·98	8·64	3·72	< 0·001
Verbal language	44·02	8·76	34·20	16·38	9·82	3·63	< 0·001
Form copying	24·97	18·59	16·73	18·82	8·24	2·24	0·05 > P > 0·02
Block design	18·33	4·90	14·20	7·68	4·13	3·15	0·01 > P > 0·002
Dependency	6·16	1·67	4·30	1·66	1·86	5·70	< 0·001
Concentration	6·01	1·67	4·45	1·93	1·56	4·35	< 0·001
Co-operation	6·13	1·67	4·68	2·24	1·45	3·64	< 0·001

Table 5 shows the social class distribution of the children studied. The groups differ in the direction of social deprivation among the cases. This was inevitable, since most of the 3-year-olds and a few of the 4-year-old cases were drawn from children born in Guy's Hospital and followed up there and they comprised children who were living within a three-mile radius of Guy's, which is mainly a working-class district of East End London.

TABLE 5. SOCIAL CLASS OF THE TWO GROUPS

	Controls		Cases	
	N	%	N	%
I and II	14	22·22	7	15·91
III	23	36·51	10	22·73
IV and V	26	41·27	27	61·36

There is a significant excess of semi-skilled and unskilled fathers (social classes IV and V) among the cases ($P < 0.05$).

Table 6 compares social class differences and the verbal tests.

TABLE 6. SOCIAL CLASS DIFFERENCES AND THE VERBAL TESTS RESULTS OF ONE-WAY ANALYSES OF VARIANCE

mean scores

	Social classes I & II	Social class III	Social classes IV & V	Frequency ratio	P
(i) *Controls*					
Verbal comprehension	49·00	44·70	37·62	16·07	0·001
Verbal language	49·14	47·87	37·85	16·64	0·001
No.	14	23	26	—	—
(ii) *Cases*					
Verbal comprehension	45·57	37·50	29·85	4·54	0·05
Verbal language	48·71	42·20	27·22	8·23	0·001
No.	7	10	27	—	—

TABLE 7. MEANS, STANDARD DEVIATIONS AND SIGNIFICANCE OF DIFFERENCE BETWEEN MEANS ON PSYCHOLOGICAL TESTS AND RATING SCALES, SEPARATELY BY SEX

| | BOYS | | | | | | | GIRLS | | | | | | |
| | 29 Controls | | 23 Cases | | Difference between means | t | F | 34 Controls | | 21 Cases | | Difference between means | t | P |
	Mean	S.D.	Mean	S.D.				Mean	S.D.	Mean	S.D.			
Age in months	44·90	—	43·13	—	1·77	0·82	NS	43·50	—	42·76	—	0·74	0·35	NS
Verbal comprehension	43·69	6·19	30·00	14·74	13·69	4·44	<0·001	41·91	8·98	38·57	11·86	3·34	1·17	NS
Verbal language	44·59	8·02	30·61	17·05	13·98	3·86	<0·001	43·53	9·45	38·14	15·04	5·39	1·62	NS
Form copying	28·17	19·50	15·78	19·90	12·39	2·23	<0·05	22·24	17·60	17·76	18·00	4·48	0·90	NS
Block design	18·41	5·58	13·74	7·51	4·67	2·54	<0·02	18·26	4·32	14·71	8·02	3·55	2·11	<0·05
Dependency	5·88	1·63	4·15	1·63	1·73	3·76	<0·001	6·40	1·69	4·45	1·72	1·95	4·10	<0·001
Concentration	5·90	1·85	4·11	2·01	1·79	3·30	<0·01	6·10	1·53	4·83	1·80	1·27	2·77	<0·01
Co-operation	6·26	1·63	4·13	2·27	2·13	3·89	<0·001	6·01	1·73	5·29	2·10	0·72	1·37	NS

Sex differences: None of the differences between the means of the control boys and the control girls reach statistically significant levels.

A further interesting point emerges from the analysis of results in Table 4. The much greater standard deviation shows that in language scores and also in the other two test scores, the cases show much greater variability than do the controls.

All the cases show greater variability than the controls. This also is a characteristic factor. A "wide spread" of successes and failures in a child's intelligence test results have, from many years' experience, alerted psychologists to the need for further exploration of such a child's difficulties.

A separate analysis of the results by sex (Table 7) showed that the perceptual tests discriminated more clearly between the boy cases and controls than between the girl cases and controls, even though the cases were matched for estimated severity of damage at birth. This is especially clear among the 3-year-olds and has some relevance to planning for learning.

The rating scales showed that the cases were significantly more dependent, had poorer concentration and were capable of poorer co-operation than the controls.

Even after making allowances for advantages or disadvantages to the child through home background; delayed language development points to a factor due to damage; and in any case, unless the child is specially helped, this will present a serious disadvantage to the child in school learning.

Self-portrait and Tactual-localization Test

The results of the research study showed both the self-portrait and the tactual localization tests to be useful pointers to deviant development, especially in the 4-year-olds.

Comparing the numbers of children in the two groups whose score on the self-portrait and on the tactual-localization test was above, below or just at the norm for their age by a chi-square test, the differences in both test results between the cases and controls was highly significant.

Self-portrait $\chi^2 = 22 \cdot 16$ d.f. $= 2$ $P = 0 \cdot 001$
Tactual localization $\chi^2 = 19 \cdot 48$ d.f. $= 2$ $P = 0 \cdot 001$

Summary of Test Results

From an examination of the test results, it is shown that the cases in this study were significantly poorer in:

1. Language development.
2. In ability to copy forms.
3. In conceptualizing, as seen through their ability to sort and match blocks according to colour, size and form.
4. In the maturity of development of self-concept.
5. On the basis of the rating scales the cases were significantly more dependent, had poorer concentration and were capable of poorer co-operation than the controls.
6. Test results of the cases generally showed wider variability than those of the controls.
7. The differences seen in the test results showed more clearly in the boy cases than in the girls, even though they were matched for severity of damage at birth.

The use of this battery of tests makes a definite contribution to our recognition and understanding of pre-school children who, through their deviant rates of development, should be regarded as possibly "at risk" of developing specific learning disorders in later school situations.

Observations Arising from Research Testing

During the course of the research testing, some observations threw interesting light on the children's methods of thinking and learning and are worthy of note.

Self-concept

A striking characteristic of the children in this age-group was the variation in their clarity of self-concept, in so far as that can be determined by their self-portraits, together with their scores on the tactual-localization test.

The concept of "body image" still remains a very controversial one. It is, however, generally recognized that there is a slowly developing awareness in the infant of himself as separate from his surroundings and that this gradually evolving self-concept becomes for the child a focus point or frame of reference, from which he reaches out to explore the world and orientate himself in space.

Writing of the anatomy and physiology of the body image in childhood, Gordon (1964) says:

> The awareness of the various parts of the body, their position in space and the relationship of one part to another is due to sensory data conveyed by a variety of channels (visual, tactual, proprioceptive from muscles and joints and labyrinthine). . . . The body image is no built-in model to be found in some specific part of the brain, but has to be laboriously acquired. Failure in its normal development, due to defects in afferent sensory pathways or to impairment of integration with the cerebrum may be an important contribution to the total disability of a handicapped child.

Woods (1958) also, describing body image as "a constant state of awareness of the position of the body", holds it to be fundamental to normal development and behaviour.

The purpose of using the self-portrait and the tactual localization test in the research described here, was to add to the test battery a further measure of the integrity of the central nervous system of the child.

While the drawing of a person by a child clearly involves his ability to manage his pencil sufficiently well to make a representational drawing, this is only one of the factors involved in the draw-a-person test. This conclusion was reached by Yule (1966) in a study of 131 children aged 9–11 years, selected at random from the total population of children of that age resident on the Isle of Wight. He found that correlation of scores assessed by the Goodenough-Harris scoring system with scores on a simple form-copying test to be only $+0\cdot30$. Although this correlation is significant at the 5 per cent level, it is low. In his very comprehensive review of the literature, Harris (1963) shows that there is little or no evidence for body-image disorder as seen in distorted body figures, missing limbs, etc., but he concludes that "a survey of the studies suggests that inconsistencies and uncertainties in execution rather than in content or in subject representation are more likely to appear in central nervous system deficit".

Out of a very wide and extensive study of children's human figure drawings, Koppitz (1968) concluded that what distinguishes the brain injured from the non-brain injured child is "primarily a malfunctioning of his integrative capacity and that this malfunctioning may result in a slower development, or incomplete or distorted functioning of perception, conceptualization, movement, expression and social behaviour". In the exploratory study of the children in the Tavistock nursery school, the human figure drawing appeared to be a very sensitive indicator of levels of development, even in this so-called normal group, and it was on this evidence that it was included in the test battery.

In the self-portrait test, there was a marked developmental factor, making the distinction more greatly significant in the 4-year-olds. By the age of 4 years, a normally developing child should have begun to form a fairly clear self-concept. It is interesting to note that only one of the 3-year-old cases could achieve a scorable response to the self-portrait test, but all the 3-year-old controls managed to do this.

While too strong a conclusion could not be drawn from such small numbers, it seemed clear from this intensive study that children who were most capable of concentration and co-operation and who were also the most independent showed the greatest clarity of self-concept, as seen from their drawings. Since there was also a highly significant difference between the cases and controls in their scores on the rating scales, it would seem to confirm the hypothesis that in so far as these drawings can be regarded as showing the child's development of self-concept or body image, the capacity to move towards self-dependence, and to concentrate attention on a given task is closely related to the development of a clear self-concept.

The developmental level in the 3-year-olds is strikingly different. Self-concept is very vague and the children were all still very dependent on mother and easily distracted by objects and pictures in the room. Two of the controls who said they could not draw

pictures of themselves chose to draw Mummy (Figs. 3 and 4).
It is interesting also to compare the progress towards clarity of
self-concept seen in the drawings in Figs. 5a and b.

Figure 5a was a boy's drawing when in the 3-year-old control
group and b is a drawing done by him in a follow-up interview
at 3 years 10 months.

FIG. 3. Picture of Mummy by 3-year-old case.

Figure 6 shows the drawing of himself by a boy aged 3 years
10 months whose rating for concentration and self-dependence,
and score for copy-forms and block sort tests placed him among
the top five children in the 4-year-old control group.

The next two drawings, shown in Figs. 7a and b were done by
the boy who ranked as the most dependent and perceptually
confused child in the 4-year-old cases. He also made the lowest
score in the tests involving visuo-spatial ability.

The first picture, Fig. 7a, was drawn when he was just 4 years

old. He constantly looked to his mother for reassurance and needed to have her very close to him while he took part in the tests.
He had great difficulty in relating the body parts to a description

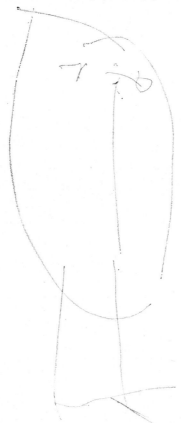

FIG. 4. Picture of Mummy by 3-year-old case.

of his own body, as can be seen in the drawing, where the body is
at the top and the ears growing from the legs and the head at the
bottom of the picture. He also made the lowest score in the tactual-
localization test.

FIG. 5a. Self-portrait by boy aged 2 years 11 months; b. self-portrait
by the same boy aged 3 years 10 months.

FIG. 5b.

At 4 years, this boy started to attend a particularly good nursery school, where he had ample opportunities for exploratory play with objects, as well as for developing his verbal skills in his communication with other children and adults.

Figure 7b shows this boy's drawing of himself 6 months later. Here, he shows not only a more organized self-concept but, drawing himself standing in front of his house, he is beginning to get some sense of orientation in space, although this time he has completely omitted the body from his self-portrait.

Perhaps the most vivid self-portrait drawn by children in this research study was the picture by Guy (Fig. 8) of himself parachuting off the climbing frame. This imaginative drawing was influenced by seeing television films of airmen parachuting. But clearly, here is a child who can orientate himself in space and also indulge in pretence and imagining.

FIG. 6. Self-portrait by boy aged 3 years and 10 months.

Movement

Observation of the children throughout the period of this study showed the importance of normal development of movement and motor co-ordination. Many of the cases were "clumsy" and unco-ordinated. This inevitably made for difficulty in all the tests that depend on drawing, but also as Woods (1958) has shown from her wide experience with cerebral palsied children, disorderly development of movement makes for difficulty in development of body image. The effect of this on learning will be discussed later.

Use of Verbalization

In this study, the children who made the highest scores in copying forms and in block sort or concept formation used language to help them in identifying their percepts. Most of the 4-year-olds could recognize and match shapes, but those who could readily copy them accurately were helped to identify their percepts and organize their ideas by active verbalizing. Luria (1961) and

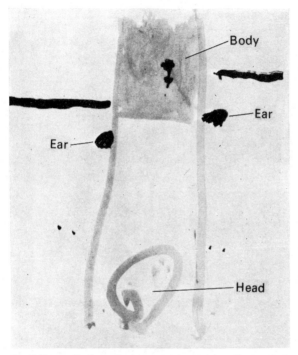

Fig. 7a. Self-portrait drawn by boy aged 4 years; b. self-portrait drawn by same boy at 4 years 6 months.

Vygotsky (1962) show how overt speech frequently accompanies purposeful action in young children. Luria describes, for example, how a child of 2 years, when asked to press a rubber bulb, will press it continuously and is not able to control the duration or frequency of pressing. At 3 years of age, however, he could learn to press it just twice, if he accompanied the pressing by verbalizing a corresponding sound pattern, such as, for example, "One, two". This integration of speech sound with movement or vision is an important factor in the development of learning in young children. The 4-year-olds, however, begin to develop the use of language for the expression of thoughts and ideas and to integrate them with new learning.

FIG. 7b.

Sheridan's (1964) distinction is pertinent here. "Speech is the use of systematized vocalizations to express verbal symbols or words. Language is the symbolization of thought, in speech, writing, drawing or gesture for the purpose of intra-personal communication and also for the purpose of storing experiences in the memory in a convenient code form."

It was their use of language as a tool of thought that distinguished the normally developing children in this age-group. This use of verbalization as an aid to thought in working out problems was demonstrated very closely by the 4-year-old boy, Guy. In doing the block sort test, he constantly verbalized while sorting or matching blocks. He was not talking to the examiner, but rather thinking aloud.

Fig. 8. Self-portrait by boy aged 3 years 11 months.

The help that he got from verbalizing was very clearly seen when he was doing the copy forms test.

In copying the inverted triangle (card 16 in copy forms) he first drew a rough circle (Fig. 9a). He was not satisfied with this and after comparing his drawing with the original, he said, "Oh! There ought to be a point at the bottom." He then drew in the "point". Still dissatisfied, he asked if he could do it all again because he had not put the points at the top. He then proceeded to put dots to show him where the points should be. Figure 9b shows his final attempt.

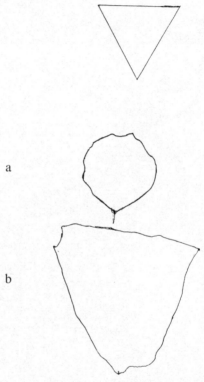

FIG. 9. Copies of card 16 in copy forms test by boy aged 3 years 11 months.

Guy's procedure was similar in his attempt to copy the diamond (card 18 in copy forms test). In this, he first drew a square and then, remarking that he had not put in the points, he put projecting lines from the square (Fig. 10a). After careful scrutiny, he remarked that the lines ought to slope from the points and he proceeded to draw "dots to show where the points are" and then he joined the dots to form the diamond (Fig. 10b).

In doing the copy forms test, many of the 4-year-olds were helped by verbalizing. It seemed for some that they must identify the form as an object before they could readily copy it. One child, looking at card 3 said, "It's a big ball and a little ball", and for card 8 he said, "The table is upside down", and for card 13, "Now the table is proper."

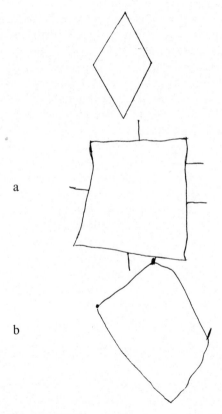

a

b

FIG. 10. Copies of card 18 in copy forms test by boy aged 3 years 11 months.

The little girl shown on Plate 2 and Fig. 2 (pp. 40, 41) adopted much the same overt reasoning procedure in carrying out that test.

Block Sort and Concept Test

The 4-year-old children found it fairly easy to form concepts in order to sort the blocks of varying shapes, colours and sizes. A further experiment was tried in which the child was asked to put a series of small toys in groups, according to how they belonged together. This was similar to the object sorting test described by Goldstein and Scheerer (1941). The objects used were all miniature toys consisting of wild animals, farm animals, furniture, kitchen utensils, people and wheeled vehicles. Only the children with the highest scores in the verbal tests managed to sort the objects on the basis of their general concept and even then, subjective and imaginative factors frequently interfered with the logic of their concepts. One boy, for example, grouped "the zoo animals", "the farm animals", "the cars, things that go on the road", and then separated a cow and calf from the farm animal group and put them together with some of the cooking pots. When asked why he grouped them in this way, he said, "Mummies and babies like to stay close together and they need something to eat out of".

One child started well, placing animals, cars and people in separate groups and then for no apparent reason, put two black cars, a black horse and a black cow in a separate group. His explanation was that "he didn't like the black things". Here we see how ego-centric children of this age still are in their thinking. Many of the children, however, simply grouped according to colour or size, without regard for the representational quality of the object.

Having decided on their basis for grouping, all the children found it extremely difficult and in many cases impossible to "shift" to another conceptual basis for sorting. This was equally difficult for them whether they were grouping the blocks in the block sort test or the small objects in the experiment described above.

The numbers of children in this research project were deliberately kept small, in order to allow of intensive study. Taking into account the intimate nature of the relationship with the children, the results appear suggestive, indicating significant trends. On these tests and rating scales the two groups of children are very clearly differentiated, more clearly in the case of the boys than the girls.

A comparison of the level of achievement between the 3- and 4-year-old controls, that is the children who are developing normally, highlights the year from 3 to 4 as one of extremely rapid development. This emphasizes the importance to children in this age range of adequate and suitable play experiences on which their minds can feed and grow. Intimate observation of the children who took part in the study showed what an important part is played by language development in the total development of the 3- and 4-year-old child. During this period of mental growth, the child begins to use language as a tool of thought, as a means of manipulating mental images, as well as for communication with other children and the people in his world.

Luria (1961) has described language as "the essential means whereby the child finds his bearings in the external world" and Lehtinen (1955) describes perception and language as constituting "the raw material of our concepts" and although a concept need not be completely verbal, she holds that it is mainly by means of language that a child by first acquiring names for them fixes the essential characteristics of his percepts. He can then use them as "schemas" which "can then be combined and recombined with a flexibility and generality far surpassing the specific situations in which they were first experienced".

Through his many experimental studies of the thinking of deaf children, Furth (1963, 1966) shows that although language is usually employed as the means of supporting the thinking of young children, it is not an absolutely essential means. It is, however, a most important tool of learning for the young normal child. For the children observed in this research study, the acquisition of the use of language at the level of verbalization would appear to be of paramount importance in the development of learning in the pre-school period. It has been shown that the level of language development, as evidenced by their scores on Reynell's tests, was significantly more mature among the controls than among the cases. The controls used language as a means to integrate their various skills.

In their experimental studies of inter-sensori patterning of cerebral palsied children, Birch and his colleagues (discussed in Chapter 2) have shown that these damaged children are significantly defective in their ability to integrate information derived from different sense modalities with one another.

Similar observations were made by Lehtinen (1955) and arose directly from her practical experience as a teacher of brain-injured children. She writes, "The organism functions as a whole. . . . The activity of one system is performed against the constant background activity of all of the others so that no perceptual or motor act occurs in isolation. What seems to happen in the brain-damaged organism is that the interactions are weaker and less translatable from one system to another."

It is this failure in integration, producing as it does an unevenness in functioning and an unstable and uncertain hold on his perceptual world that, for the present writer at any rate, is the major signal that the child is likely to be in trouble. This shows itself in various ways. Among the group of 3-year-old cases in the research study, those children whose outstanding development of verbal ability contrasts so strikingly with their poor achievement on all the other tests are examples of children who should be identified and helped. Two of the most striking of such cases are described in Chapter 4. It is important not to be misled by facile and easy speech to overlook the capacity for integration in all areas of functioning, a capacity to which the use of language as a tool of thought should be progressively contributing in these early pre-school years.

There are other pointers to poor capacity for integration in young children. Lehtinen (1955) suggests that "much of the awkwardness of the brain-damaged child appears to be due to a lack of integration of perceptual and motor systems as well as the failure of the visual perceptual processes to provide substantial and clearly structured patterns for the motor actions to follow". Clumsiness in movement as well as distractibility greater than can be reasonably expected in young children should alert those caring for them to the possibility that they need extra help.

Delayed or retarded development of speech and language is rightly regarded in itself by doctors and teachers as an early and indeed a very sensitive indicator that a child is in difficulties.

The results of this research study, combined with careful observation of the children throughout the time indicate that the following should be regarded as signals that a child, at 3–5 years, is showing dysfunction or deviant development that could produce specific learning difficulties in school:

(I) Language development—(a) Lack of clarity in speech even in communication with familiar teachers and children whom they regard as "friends", (b) clear speech articulation, but the failure to use language as a symbolic process and to integrate its use into the performance of other learning tasks.

(II) Difficulties in visuo-spatial perception—seen in difficulty in such tasks as judging distance of real objects in their environment, difficulties in orientation, in recognizing position, sorting and matching according to shape, copying forms, reproducing structures built in bricks.

(III) Motor development—(a) Clumsiness and awkwardness of movement, bumping into and knocking over and spilling things, (b) difficulties of praxis—putting on shoes and coats, tying shoe laces and fastening buttons, (c) delayed sense of body image.

(IV) More than normal distractibility and limited attention span.

If, in spite of help and opportunities for extra experience and exploration of objects in his environment, the child makes little progress and particularly if he remains grossly uneven in his levels of development, as well as restless and distractible, this would warrant the referral for further investigation.

The psychologist's contribution to the diagnostic investigation, together with suggestions of ways of helping these various children, will be discussed in the next chapter.

CHAPTER 4

Helping Children
Before Starting Formal School

THIS chapter is concerned with young children likely to be brought to notice because they are developing unevenly and are showing delayed development in some areas important to learning.

It is part of the psychologist's responsibility firstly to make a careful diagnostic assessment of the child's level of functioning, of his assets as well as his liabilities, and secondly to guide the parents and nursery school teachers by suggesting ways of helping the child to overcome his difficulties, in preparation for a more successful school experience.

Psychologists working with young children make their own choice of tests with which they are experienced and which they have found to be useful tools for the purpose of differential diagnosis of the child's problem.

There are many admirable surveys of tests and their applicability to various purposes, such as the work of Anastasi (1961), Cronbach (1960) and Vernon (1960). A very useful review and evaluation of infant and pre-school mental tests is presented by Stott and Ball (1965). This is a most comprehensive survey and for those psychologists who seek to improve on ways of making diagnostic assessments of young children, a study of this monograph will prove to be invaluable. For those who are not experienced in assessment of handicapped children, the works of Taylor (1959) and Haeussermann (1958) give many insights gained from wide clinical experience.

In making a diagnostic assessment, it is generally helpful first to gain as accurate a measure as possible of the child's overall level of intellectual functioning at the time, bearing in mind that the predictive value of pre-school scales for normal young children is by no means established. It is a help, however, to get a picture of the child's *present* level of functioning. Tests of young children measure different groups of functions at successive age levels. Various aspects of development and behaviour are all facets of total mental growth, but although these functions all contribute to what we understand as intelligent behaviour, they are really a series of developing functions, each growing out of a previously matured behaviour pattern.

In testing, it is important to remember that young children are much more at the mercy of their inner fantasies and their emotional mood than are school-age children. They are also much more totally affected by their state of well-being at the time of testing.

All the difficulties inherent in testing young children are exaggerated in the testing of neurologically handicapped children. These children frequently present a wide scatter in their level of abilities. They are generally more anxious, more quickly fatiguable and their attention span is often much shorter than is that of a normal young child.

In choice and use of tests with these children, therefore, as much as possible should be known about the developmental history, health record, results of medical and neurological examinations, the attitude of the parents to the child, the emotional climate of his home and the opportunities for intellectual stimulation. With handicapped young children even more than others, the presence of the mother during the test can be of positive value. By observing the mother and child together, a great deal can be learnt about the emotional quality of the mother–child relationship. It is frequently the case that the mother provides a bridge of communication between the examiner and the child, when the child's speech is poor, or when the child is too afraid at first to take instruction from a stranger.

Because we are concerned with children whose problem is related to unevenness of development, it is important, even though formal intelligence tests are used, not to be satisfied with a result presented merely in the form of a global I.Q. rating. In her account of psychological appraisal of children with cerebral defects, Taylor (1959) shows vividly how much a meaningful "appraisal" can contribute to suitable planning for helping the child who has been assessed. In reaching her decisions regarding suitable plans, she combines test items that lend themselves to objective and quantifiable treatment with others that depend on psychological experience and intuition. In seeking to assess the educational potential of handicapped pre-school children and indeed of children whose deviant development raises the question of possible psychoneurological learning disorder, the careful work of Haeussermann (1958) offers many useful insights and merits study.

Of the forty-four cases in the research study described in the previous chapter, all of whom had been noted at birth as having some minor neurological dysfunction, five boys and three girls were so severely damaged that they would be unlikely to be capable of benefitting from formal school teaching. Tested before school age, this group were all of I.Q. below 50, using the L-M Revision of the Stanford-Binet Scale; ten boys and one girl fell into the group of I.Q. range 60–75. Of the remaining cases, seventeen children ranged in I.Q. from 80 to 110; of these, there were six boys and eleven girls. Also, there were eight children—four boys and four girls—with I.Q.'s ranging from 115 to 120.

These children were all tested on the Stanford-Binet, just before they reached 5 years of age. The testing was not carried out by the same examiner who had individually tested the children in the research proper, and was not formally a part of the research project.

Our concern in the research study had been to investigate the possibility of identifying children who, though of normal intelligence, showed indications that they would have learning difficulties later. It was thought that the best pointers would lie in evidence of marked deviations in development during the early developmental years; in fact examination of the results of the battery of tests used in the research project proper showed that a number of children had marked differences in their rates of development. The test results were grouped into verbal and performance tests, which combined the results on copy form, block sort and self-concept. A difference between the results of the tests, grouped in this way, was regarded as significant if it was as great as two standard deviations.

Of the children chosen as meriting further investigation in view of the unevenness of development, there were nine in the average group and seven in the above-average group. These children were singled out for further investigation as soon as their research test results became available. Of these, six girls and two boys had verbal test scores significantly higher than their performance test scores and three girls and five boys had significantly lower verbal test scores.

It was not possible to make a careful investigation of all the forty-four children, but for those who showed no marked unevenness in achievement in the test battery a school report or, on four occasions, a visit to the child's school and discussion with their teachers, confirmed that they did not have any learning problems that had brought them to special notice.

The eighteen children whose unevenness of development made it seem likely that they might have learning difficulties were seen again for individual assessment, as soon as it was possible after the original research study was completed.

While it was clearly not practical to formulate a carefully planned research design to assess the value of training methods to help these children, some attempt was made to give guidance and advice either to parents and/or nursery school teachers, where the child was attending nursery school.

Children with Visuo-spatial and Motor Disability

The following examples are taken from two children in the study who fall into this category.

Case 1. Paul. This boy had been noted at birth as having minor neurological dysfunction following the mother's long labour and deep forceps delivery.

He was taken into the study at 3 years of age. Seen at that time he was an anxious, timid boy, extremely dependent on his parents. He was mildly clumsy in walking and his fine motor control was poor. He did very badly in the form copying test. He did not make any score on self-portrait and his score on tactual-localization was low. His result on the block sort test, was, however, average for his age. His results on the verbal tests, both for comprehension and expressive language, were very much above average for his age.

This boy's parents were both trained teachers and they were ready and interested to discuss Paul's assets and disabilities. They were able to understand that he could be helped by giving him a wide range of experience in sensori-motor skills and that this could be best fostered by calling his good language ability into the service of his other learning. They readily grasped the idea of his need for help in integrating his use of language with the development of other visuo-spatial skills, in which up to that time he was retarded. Paul's parents were particularly understanding and co-operative and they had the good sense to see that real help also involved building up in Paul a sense of successful achievement, without subjecting him to undue pressure.

This family had moved from London and lived then in the North of England, but so great was their enthusiasm and interest that they asked if they could bring him back at 4 years old for a further assessment and advice.

When he came at 4 years, he was tested on the Wechsler Preschool and Primary Scale of Intelligence (for description of the test see Chapter 5). His score on this test was Verbal Scale I.Q. 116, Performance Scale I.Q. 115, Full Scale I.Q. 117. The performance scale contained a test of copying geometric designs, a test of simple mazes, and simple block designs, all types of task which he would have found difficult, in comparison with the verbal tests a year previously. Paul came back, again at the parent's own request, at 5 years. He was then just about to start school. He had gained in every way, scoring well above average in all tests and also showing a very great advance in self-confidence and self-dependence. He had already begun to read and was looking forward to starting school. A recent letter from his parents reported that he has now settled happily at school and is doing well.

This child had very real advantages in his home background and the interested help without pressure that his parents could give him.

Contrast this with

Case 2. Susan. Susan had anoxic hypotonia at birth. Her performance at the 3-years'-old examination was very similar to that of Paul. She was timid and anxious and depended throughout the test interview on her mother's presence and repeated reassurance. Like Paul, her walking and her fine motor co-ordination were poor. She did very badly on form copying and indeed had great difficulty in managing to use a pencil at all. She could make no attempt at self-portrait and had only very limited success on tactual-localization. Her score on the block sort test was also well below average for her age. Her results on both the verbal tests were above average.

Susan came from a very poor home where her mother, deserted by her husband soon after Susan's birth, struggled on very limited means to bring up a large family. She was very devoted to Susan and did not wish her to start school until she was 5.

Susan was seen again for a follow-up at 4 years and she had made just the progress expected of normal developmental maturing. The variability characteristic of her earlier achievement remained. Here was an extremely "disadvantaged" child who was lacking the kind of help Paul was so fortunate in having. It was felt in the hospital at this time that Susan needed physiotherapy to help to overcome, or at any rate minimize, her very real motor handicap and it was then possible to help her mother to recognize the advantage that it would be to Susan to allow her to attend a small nursery school nearby. The teacher of this school was interested in trying to give Susan extra experience in the kind of sensory and play materials, which would help her to overcome her visuo-motor disabilities and she valued and acted upon any suggestions that we could make. Seen again at 5 years, just prior to starting school, Susan had made considerable progress. She was tested on the Wechsler Pre-school and Primary Scale with the following results—Verbal Scale I.Q. 110, Performance Scale I.Q. 89, Full Scale I.Q. 100. The gap between her visuo-motor skills and verbal ability showed that she still had considerable unevenness of development and it is possible that she might have bridged this gap more successfully if she had had the benefit of extra help during the crucial 3–4 year.

Children with Language Disabilities

An examination of the eight cases in the research study whose language development was low, in relation to their visuo-spatial abilities, showed a much more confused picture. There seemed to be many varied reasons for their language delay.

The following cases are chosen to illustrate this.

Case 1. Cedric. (aged 4 years). This boy had a severe executive aphasia. At 4 years, he had an almost complete inability to use language as a means of expression and communication. Although it seemed from his behaviour in a test situation that his understanding of language was also seriously limited, in the carefully standardized situation of Reynell's Verbal Test procedure, his score on the comprehension of language was within normal limits, although towards the lower end of "normal", but he made virtually no score on the expressive language test. His condition would seem to be one of congenital auditory imperception or, as it is rather misleadingly designated, "central deafness".

In the copy forms, and the block sort, his achievement was high in the normal range. His mother was advised each day to give him her undivided time in a period of conversation, when she would have him on her knee and converse with him at "mother distance" as Sheridan (1964) has so aptly described it. He was placed also in a day nursery school for children with his condition, most of whom were partially deaf.

There, he did well and on reaching 5 years of age, it was decided that he could take his place in a normal primary school. In the infants department, where the classes were small and the teachers could devote time and care to him, he seemed to manage normally well. He was also helped by good speech therapy of the kind described so vividly by Renfrew (1964). As this boy is reaching the stage when formal learning is beginning to play a more important part, he is progressively finding school life and achievement more difficult. Although he appears to have only slight hearing loss, so that he could be regarded as capable of functioning within the normal range, he obviously needs a more special kind of teaching help, probably in a much smaller group and at a slower pace. This type of child, although identified early as likely to have learning difficulties, has difficulties which are not yet wholly understood and for which it is still difficult to find the best methods of catering.

This boy was, without exception, the most problematic "speech disorder" child of the cases studied.

Case 2. David (age 4 years, 1 month). This boy is chosen here for description because he presents also a condition due to birth injury. David was quick and competent in carrying out all the non-verbal tests in the research study test battery and his whole approach to the test situation suggested that he was a boy of high intelligence. On Reynell's Verbal Comprehension Test, where responses by pointing and manipulating the test material without the need to use speech are acceptable, he made a score above his chronological age level.

David, however, had a severe speech disorder, which made his articulation so poor as to be virtually incomprehensible. This boy was examined by an otologist and his disorder of speech production was diagnosed as being caused by a structural malformation of the palate. This was corrected by surgical operation, followed by speech therapy. Gradually, the loss caused by David's early disorder of speech production was bridged and with intensive speech training that also involved extended use of language, he was able to hold a place in school in keeping with his good intelligence.

These two cases are exceptional and for the major number of the children in this study whose language development was delayed, in comparison with their achievement on the non-verbal tests, it was not easy to find an explanation in any way related to their classification at birth of having possible "minor neurological damage".

Of the children in the study who were globally subnormal in intelligence, only one had a marked deviation in some areas of development and since we are concerned in this study with children of normal intelligence who are showing signs of being likely to have specific learning disabilities, a discussion of the subnormal child falls outside its scope.

It should, however, be remarked in passing that of the twenty-five cases of average or above-average intelligence, nine showed no evidence of possible learning disabilities at 4 years of age and by the age of 5 years, three of the children for whom extra help had been arranged would not have been picked out in school as needing extra help.

These results are interesting in the light of the follow-up at 7 years by Corah et al. (1965) of the children who had been studied at birth and at 3 years of age (Graham, et al., 1962, Graham et al., 1960) for the effects of perinatal anoxia. The assumption in these various investigations is that anoxia produces brain damage and that this effect is detectable at all age levels. Knobloch and Pasamanick (1959) have postulated a "continuum of reproductive casualty", as resulting from complications of the perinatal period. It is the extreme of the continuum represented by a "syndrome of minimal cerebral damage" that is the more difficult to delineate. This concept of a minimal brain damage syndrome has, however, received support by a number of writers, such as Gesell and Amatruda (1941) and Paine (1962).

In this follow-up, the effects of perinatal anoxia were studied in a group of 7-year-old children, who had also been examined at birth and 3 years of age. The follow-up sample was composed of

134 children who were normal, full-term newborns and 101 children who were anoxic full-term new-borns. This 235 children represented 85·5 per cent of the selected sample which had been studied at 3 years of age. The anoxic group was composed of three sub-groups—those with signs of perinatal anoxia, those with post-natal apnœa and those with signs of both conditions.

The follow-up was conducted without knowledge of the new-born classification and included assessment in the areas of cognitive and perceptual functioning, of personality and of neurological impairment.

The results of this study showed that there was no longer a significant deficit in intelligence in the anoxic group. The only test of cognitive function on which the anoxics demonstrated a significant deficit was the vocabulary sub-test from the W.I.S.C. This result was interpreted in terms of a deficit in abstract ability. The anoxics also obtained significantly lower scores on a test of perceptual motor functioning and they tended to do poorly on a special test of perceptual attention.

While the study suggests that perinatal anoxia is related to deficits evident at 7 years of age, it was also evident that such deficits which do occur are reasonably minimal for the group as a whole. While the degree of impairment tended to be associated with new-born criteria of severity, the association was a weak one. A prognosis for any given new-born would be very difficult to make, except when there are very severe or numerous complications.

In the research study described in the previous chapter, although some of the children showed no evidence of disorderly mental development which might have resulted from known signs of minor neurological damage in early infancy, there were marked significant differences between test results and rating scales of the controls and the cases among some of the children. Of the forty-four cases, eighteen per cent were severely subnormal. These were children who had also severe physical damage. Twenty five per cent of the group would need educational provision as educationally sub-normal children. Although most of these children were globally low in all areas of performance, some showed unevenness of achievement which might lead to possible specific learning disabilities in some school subject. The main concern of the study, however, was an investigation into the identification and possible ways of helping pre-school children of normal intelligence, who from deviant development in pre-school years, might have later learning difficulties.

Of the forty-four cases, 57 per cent of the children were of average or above average intelligence and of these children, 64 per cent showed deviant development in some areas of testing and/or behavioural characteristics, which pointed to the need for help before starting school.

Experiments in helping Pre-school Children whose Deviant Rates of Development Point to Possibility of Later Learning Disabilities

At the time of writing, I know of no carefully designed research study into the best methods of training the pre-school child to help bridge the gaps caused by unevenness in development, thought to be caused by neurological impairment in early infancy.

Many experimental approaches to helping these children are being made and they will be discussed here and evaluated as far as this is possible at the present time.

The learning difficulties which would seem to arise from psycho-neurological impairment fall into the following main categories:

1. *Difficulties Arising from Disorderly Development of Perceptual and Visuo-motor Skills*

These disorders are seen variously as difficulties in recognizing shapes and patterns, reproducing patterns and shapes from memory or even from a copy, copying simple structures built in bricks or putting together very simple jig-saws. There is frequent difficulty in recognizing position, left and right, above and below, in front of and behind.

In seeking to help young cerebral palsied children to overcome these difficulties, it has been thought that a good nursery school, by making available to such handicapped children all those early childhood play experiences essential for children's normal growth would make it possible for these damaged children to "make up" for their loss. Many such schools plan imaginative ways by which the child can extend his experience in relation to form, size, texture and weight. Writing of her experience in a school for cerebral palsied children, Caldwell (1956) says:

> The pre-school experiences of tasting, hearing, handling, pushing and pulling, rolling, crawling, bumping and banging . . . are necessary parts of a normal infant's development. Further experimentation with stones, soil, sand and water and play with dolls and other simple toys, with other children and a loving understanding grown-up in the background form the vital preparation for school life. Through these early experiences a normal toddler receives valuable sensory training.

In her school for cerebral palsied children, however, Caldwell noticed that many of the older children who had developed mentally beyond a "baby play" stage had not acquired sensory experiences. Many of these children had sufficient physical mobility to gain these experiences at the right age and stage of mental development, but they had not acquired that degree of spatial perception that is necessary before a child can "dress himself, understand a picture, draw even a symbolic shape, let alone tackle the more intricate arts of learning to read and write letters or figures. Yet many of these children were otherwise intelligent".

It was clear that simply to offer extended nursery school experience was not enough for these perceptually handicapped children. In order to help them, Caldwell had to offer a very carefully planned and graded course of training, geared to the particular difficulties of each individual child. She describes in vivid detail her method, as adapted to the needs of one particular case. While this admirable work was very successful with certain children, it does not lend itself to a research study of the merits or demerits of the methods she adopted.

Among the most formally designed plans for giving these

perceptually damaged children special help was that worked out by Albitreccia in Paris. Between 1945 and her death in 1960, Madame Albitreccia worked with Dr. Auguste Tournay at the Aide aux Enfants Paralysés Centre in Paris, where she developed many new ideas and novel approaches in her attempts to overcome sensori-motor and speech disorders of children handicapped by polio and cerebral palsy.

Madame Albitreccia believed that in these handicapped children, disorders of body image were really at the root of their early learning problems. She said, "Problems that arise when a child enters school and manifest themselves as perceptual difficulties are rooted in faulty body image and often have nothing whatever to do with his intellectual capacities. They are a direct manifestation of the correlation that exists between disturbances of the body image and spatial difficulties transferred to the scholastic plane".

Whether or not one could go all the way with that view, I think we would all agree from our own observation of infants that there is a slowly developing awareness by the infant of himself as separate from his surroundings and that this gradually evolving self-concept becomes a focus point or frame of reference for the child, from which he reaches out to explore the world and orientate himself in space.

Most of her remedial work with young children was based on that premise. She developed a number of exercises to help these children. She has described these very fully in her paper *Recognition and Treatment of Disturbances of the Body Image* (1958).

Her remedial exercises fall into three main groups:

1. Those concerned with perception and movement. In this group, great emphasis is placed on the value of exercises to develop awareness of the body and its parts and practice in making bodily movements.
2. Those concerned with speech and language.
3. Those directly relevant to the beginning of formal school learning—particularly preparation for the beginnings in reading and writing.

Albitreccia started her career as a speech therapist and she was very conscious of the need for integration of speech therapy with training in bodily awareness. In many of the exercises designed to train perception and movement, the child was also required to verbalize what he was doing.

Her work was with severely handicapped cerebral palsied children, but many of her ideas are being adopted and tried with children whose deviant development would seem to arise from organic neurological impairment.

Among them are exercises in reconstructing a picture of a human face from separate features and also in reconstructing a human figure. Simple movements are then copied and repeated on a manikin.

She also made use of exercises to develop shape and colour discrimination, copying designs on a peg-board, as well as many exercises designed to help a child to realize position with regard to self, such as, for example, right–left, up–down, above–below.

Madame Albitreccia believed that pre-school children whose development of form perception was lagging behind their language development could be helped by extra opportunities to gain more sensory experiences and greater recognition of position in space. Much of this experience was best gained through practice with objects and in conversation with people regarding what the child was doing and noticing. She also gave the children constant and graded practice in sorting and matching shapes, colours and sizes, practice in copying structures built in bricks, or in making simple jig-saw pictures.

Although teachers and psychologists have borrowed parts of Albitreccia's method, up to this date, I know of no one in this country who has experimented with the whole of her scheme as a formal research project to assess its value.

Madame Ghislane le Borne (1965) in Brussels uses it in the same way as Albitreccia herself and has described it in detail in *A Training Method for Reducing Perceptual Disorders*. An interesting description and evaluation of Albitreccia's work is also given by Graham (1965) in *Teaching the Cerebral Palsied Child*.

Albitreccia was herself a very vivid personality and it is difficult to separate the value of the training programme she evolved from the influence of herself as a person on the children she served. She herself believed that her training scheme was effective, but there is room for more careful research study into the validity of effectiveness of her exercises. It would be useful to know how far each exercise in her programme was effective independently of the others, how far it does what it is claimed to do and whether there is evidence of transfer of training.

Another question that is raised by an intensive training programme of this sort is what is the optimum age for beginning this kind of training? Writing of *Disturbances of the Body Image*, Ritchie Russell (1958) noted that "when infantile hemiplegia comes on before the child is eighteen months of age there is a considerable capacity for one hemisphere to develop some control of the limbs on the same side as the brain damage, so much so that severe degrees of hemi-loss of body image are not observed in cases of hemiplegia of many years' standing which developed in infancy".

This suggests that corrective training should be given to the child when quite young, if it is to be effective. It is part of Albitreccia's thesis that if such training in bodily movements is effective, it will also be seen in the child's greater ability to cope with educational tasks. Albitreccia's greatest contribution to finding ways of helping to reduce perceptual difficulties in young children was, I believe, her recognition of the need to help the child to *integrate* his use of language with his development of visuo-spatial ability and his bodily awareness. My own observation of the 3 and 4 year-olds in my research study emphasized for me the major importance of integration of skills to lead to the total development of each.

2. *Children with Poor Motor Co-ordination*

Many of the forty-four cases in the research study group would be characterized as "clumsy" children. They were awkward in learning to dress themselves and to handle a spoon and fork to feed themselves. Their manual dexterity was poor. Writing from her experience in the Bristol Nursery School for Cerebral Palsied Children, of the importance of movement in the development of a body image, Dr. Woods (1958) says:

> We are becoming conscious that these spastic children need all the movement and freedom of movement thay can get. They need to experiment with sand, water, etc., at a very early age. They must crawl and roll whenever possible and should learn to feel their own bodies and the bodies of other people. They should learn to dress and undress and the physiotherapist can help by making the child conscious of all his movements. We feel that many of our children have benefited considerably by this movement and this is one of the reasons why admission at as early an age as 3 years is beneficial.

Though I know of no research studies which formally assess the value of extended experience for mildly damaged children during pre-school years, observation of the small number of cases for whom it was possible to arrange attendance at good nursery school suggested that the children were greatly helped by being given opportunities to gain experience in tactile activities— matching different materials by touch, picking out those that feel the same, things that feel soft and things that feel rough and "scratchy". Finger painting also affords good practice in controlling hand movements and the child who could not draw, even when using a thick pencil or crayon, was greatly helped by having his hand guided until he could manage the movements without help. If these children had not been given extra help before starting formal school, their inability to draw and to write and copy, as well as their clumsiness in movement and awkwardness in games, would not only have interfered with their educational progress but also have given rise to much frustration and sense of failure.

The contrast between the levels of perceptual ability in the 3- and 4-year-old children in the research study described in the previous chapter is very striking indeed. This emphasizes the importance of knowing what is reasonable and possible for young children of different ages. Many parents, in their eagerness that their child should "get on" well when he starts school, set him tasks that are quite outside the range of what is possible at his stage of perceptual development. A 3-year-old in the research study group, when asked to draw a picture of himself, Jonathon, simply filled the page with a line of scribble. His mother explained that he was writing Jonathon and she then said, "Now do Mummy," and he did another scribble. She said, "He is trying to write Mummy," and continued to describe how every day, she tried to teach him to write, "with chalk on his own blackboard". Clearly, this child was being given tasks by his mother that were beyond his capacity and that were not meaningful at his age.

Observations of the difficulties in visuo-spatial perception encountered by certain groups of cerebral palsied children—difficulties which make for quite severe learning problems—have helped to arouse greater interest in the course and pattern of the development of visuo-spatial perception in normal children. Most studies are concerned with children who have already started school, but a few studies of certain aspects of perceptual development in young children are of some interest and significance. In 1955, Elizabeth Newson made a careful study of the development of line figure discrimination in pre-school children. The study was aimed at assessing the ability of children on entry to the infant's school to discriminate between orientational variations of meaningless line figures. Newson found that at the age of 5 years, the children showed considerable difficulty in discriminating between a line figure and its mirror image, although at that age, they could discriminate fairly reliably between the line figure and other orientational variations of it.

It is of interest that she found the disability to bear no relation to handedness and that it had only a very low correlation with intelligence, as assessed by the Stanford–Binet Scale. Newson found the disability to be particularly pronounced where the line figures concerned fall into certain categories with reference to symmetry. In this category are included such letters as S, N, and Z. As part of her study, Newson initiated a training procedure for a group of nursery school children aged 4–4½ years in the ability to show perceptual discrimination of this kind. The performance in her discrimination test by the trained group of younger children was significantly better than that of the untrained group of 5-year-olds and Newson concluded from her study that the existence of the disability at 5 years must be taken as due entirely to lack of experience in the concept involved. She found evidence also that reading and writing progress during the first year at school depends more upon the early acquisition of the ability to make use of this concept than upon intelligence.

In his studies of perceptual-motor development and shape discrimination and shape copying in young children, Wedell (1964 and 1965) found that training in shape discrimination was effective for infant school children of $5\frac{1}{4}$ years old, but not for nursery school children of $3\frac{1}{4}$ years. Although there were wide individual differences in performance, most of the nursery children were not yet able to make some of the discriminations. Wedell held that this was not due to poor visual acuity, but rather that the differences in the patterns were not meaningful to children of that age. This raised the question as to whether or not the differences could have been made more meaningful by using a different training method, since an analysis of the children's pattern copying suggested that the pattern copy may be poor, not because the visual discrimination required is beyond him, but rather because he has not understood the level of accuracy that is required of him. Wedell concludes:

> This is likely to be true of a proportion of children showing impaired perceptual-motor performance and it is obviously important to distinguish these from the others "who cannot make their hands do what their eyes (in fact) see". The distorted visual experience of many cerebral palsied children may well result in habits of observation which miss out aspects of visual discrimination which are vital for pattern copying and perceptual-motor tasks in general.

These studies raise quite important questions regarding early identification and possible method of training children who are showing difficulty in this area of development.

Ghent has made interesting contributions to our understanding of perceptual development of young children in a number of research studies. In 1961, she made a study of the influence of orientation on young children's perception of form. She chose as subjects for her study children ranging in age from 4 to 8 years. She used two series of five pairs of pictures; in the first series, pictures of a rooster, flowerpot, shoe, cat and chair and in the final series, pictures of a tree, boat, cup, clown and horse. Between these two series, she showed a series of sixteen pairs of "non-realistic" or non-representational geometric figures. The children were shown each pair of pictures and asked to show which one was upside down or wrong. The pre-school children showed remarkably consistent preferences for a particular orientation of the non-realistic figures and made their choices with the same speed and ease which they had shown with the representational forms. The children of over 6 years usually hesitated when the non-realistic forms were presented and were frequently reluctant to make a choice, saying, "It doesn't matter", or "I can't tell". An analysis of the young children's preferences indicated that the young child prefers the focal part of the form to be in the upper portion of the figure and that in the development of form-perception, scanning of form proceeds in a downward direction. Ghent suggests that for a young child, a geometric form is considered right side up when the position of the form on the card conforms to or reinforces the preferred sequence of scanning and that this confirms the views of Hebb and Piaget, in contradiction to the Gestalt view that perception of simple forms shows genetic development. In older children and in adults, judgement of the orientation of a form is usually thought to be based on the relation of the position of a particular figure to the position of other figures in the environment or the frame surrounding the figure. On the other hand, this study suggests that for the young child, the judgement may be based on whether the position of the form facilitates or conflicts with movement-tendencies of the child and in the development of form-perception, scanning of form proceeds in a downward direction.

Figure 11 shows the percentage of boys and girls in each age-group choosing the card as upside down in the orientation shown.

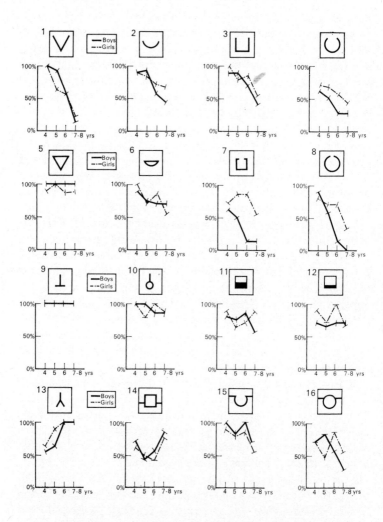

FIG. 11. Percentage of boys and girls in each age-group choosing cards as upside down in the orientation shown. (Form and its orientation: a child's eyeview, Lila Ghent, *American Journal of Psychology*, **74**, 177–190 (1961), University of Illinois Press.)

Ghent (1956) has also made a careful study of the perception of overlapping and embedded figures by children between the ages of 4 and 13 years. The perception of figures that are not clearly set apart from each other is a perceptual task that has been reported to present special difficulty to brain-injured patients and

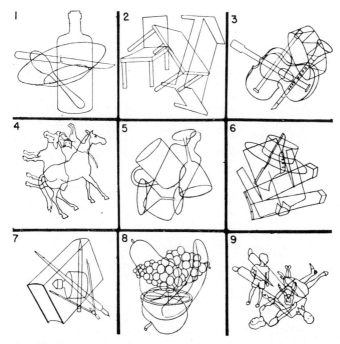

FIG. 12. Overlapping realistic figures. (Perception of overlapping and embedded figures by children of different ages, Lila Ghent, *American Journal of Psychology*, **60**, 755–587 (1956), University of Illinois Press.)

to young normal children. Ghent made two experiments. In the first, she used pictures which consisted of overlapping line drawings of various objects and she asked the children to tell her what they saw in the picture (Fig. 12).

She found that the children made very few omissions even at

the youngest age-group, and that there was a consistent decline in the number of omissions with increasing age. An analysis of the errors in response to individual items raise the following questions: Was the good performance in unscrambling the overlapping figures due to the presentation of relatively familiar objects? Was it related to the fact that the figures were overlapping, rather than embedded? Was the improvement in performance

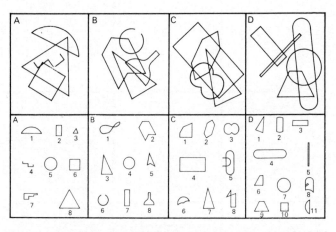

FIG. 13. Overlapping geometric figures. (Perception of overlapping and embedded figures by children of different ages, Lila Ghent, *American Journal of Psychology*, **69**, 575–587 (1956), University of Illinois Press.)

with increasing age due primarily to increasing capacity to recognize and to name line drawings?

In order to try to clarify some of these questions, Ghent set up a second experiment, in which comparisons were made between realistic and geometric overlapping figures and between overlapping and embedded figures. In order to reduce the effect of the ability to identify and name line drawings in producing improvement with age, she used a multiple-choice method of response with the geometric overlapping figures.

In this experiment, she used three series. For series A, cards

1, 6, 8 and 9 were used from the cards shown in Fig. 12 for the previous experiment. Series B is shown in Fig. 13. In this, the child is asked to find on the large sheet showing multiple-choice items all the pictures he saw on the smaller cards, each card, A, B, C, and D shown separately. Series C consisted of embedded geometric figures taken from Thurstone's modification of the Gottschaldt figures (Fig. 14).

In this, the child is shown the simple figure and is then asked to trace the part that looks exactly like it in the more complex

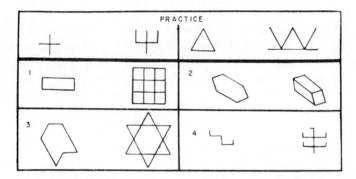

FIG. 14. Embedded geometric figures. (Perception of overlapping and embedded figures by children of different ages, Lila Ghent, *American Journal of Psychology*, **69**, 575–587 (1956), University of Illinois Press.)

figure. In this test, two practice figures were used. This series of tests was given to children ranging in age from 4 to 8 years. For the overlapping figures, both realistic and geometric, the number of omissions was found to be small, even for the youngest group. Significantly more errors were made with the embedded figures, though here again, performance improved with age. The child's difficulty with the embedded figures was greatest when the boundaries of the forms coincided with other figures and this difficulty appeared to be much greater than when the boundaries only intersected those of other figures. Ghent suggested that the improvement with age reflects an increase in the capacity to perceive a boundary as belonging to more than one figure and this she believes to be consistent with the fact that young children have a narrow perceptual span, so that a relatively restricted number of lines may be seen simultaneously and remembered, after the eyes have shifted to another spot. She says, "The capacity to see and remember a certain number of lines at any one moment would presumably have to reach a certain level of development before the child would be able to perceive a given line as belonging to more than one form".

The type of research studies described above contribute to our understanding of early development of perception in young children and therefore have some relevance to approaches to the beginning of teaching. They also emphasize the importance of the fact that any help we give these children by means of extra training practice or extended experience through play exercises must be given within a recognition of what is reasonable and possible for them at their own particular level of maturation and learning capacity.

3. *The Distractible Child*

It was seen in the research study that the cases were significantly more distractible than the controls, assessed by the rating scale. Cruickshank (1968) defines this kind of distractibility as "sensory hyperactivity". There is considerable controversy regarding the best way to help children to overcome this behavioural characteristic in a learning situation. In order to help a child to concentrate and, as he terms it, "to refrain from reacting to inessential stimuli", he believes that the child should be taught in a completely stimulus-free environment. He says, "In an ideal classroom, walls, furniture, woodwork and floor covering would be all the same colour. Windows would have opaque glass to reduce stimuli outside the building. The ceiling would be sound treated and the floor would have wall-to-wall carpeting. Shelves would be behind wooden doors. Every effort would be made to have the environment surrounding the learner as stimulus-free as possible." He also believes that the classroom for hyperactive children should be smaller than the traditional one and that small cubicles for each child should be provided within the classroom, so that the child can readily orientate himself in space.

Cruickshank is discussing here the problems of catering for the school-age child. While it is often necessary, as was so well demonstrated originally by Strauss and Lehtinen (1947) in the Cove Schools, Illinois, to make concentration possible for these children by strongly reducing environmental stimuli, there is some controversy as to the extent to which we should protect these children from distraction. Our goal is to help these children to live and learn in conditions resembling as nearly as possible a normal school community. It is important, therefore, to watch for opportunities for a progressive introduction of stimuli for the child, though there will probably always be times when a child needs a quiet corner in which to concentrate.

I believe this to be important in the pre-school years. Visiting a nursery school for children with cerebral palsy attached to the Children's Hospital in Boston, I was impressed by the pictures, the play material and interesting decorations, that made the room appear like any normal nursery. The helpers all wore brightly coloured flower-patterned overalls. The Head held very strong opinions about this.

She believed that young children should be allowed to begin their social and intellectual learning in as normal an environment as possible. But I could not help observing how watchful she was of these children under her care. When she noticed a child withdrawing from the group and dreaming, she quickly made a new contact with the child and, as it were, brought him back to his real world through her own warmth and affection. Similarly, when the pressures and stimulation of the environment were obviously too disrupting to a child, she gave him an opportunity to carry out a simple and clearly defined task in what she described as "a quiet corner where he could collect himself again". I noticed, too, that she herself or a helper would always stay with the child. She was a very remarkable woman and it seemed to me that in this setting, she was able to strike a healthy balance between quietness and freedom from distractions and the quite valuable stimulation of group activities and interests, because too much freedom from environmental stimulation can itself be detrimental to concentration. We have seen in the study by Schaffer (1958) of babies under 7 months of age who had been in hospital for periods of 1–2 weeks, that on removal from hospital they appeared to be almost unaware of objects and people, even their mothers, and spent their time gazing round with blank, bewildered expressions. This behaviour seemed to have been caused by the prolonged exposure to monotonous and unchanging surroundings, where they could see little and were seldom nursed or talked to. They were described as having become "rigidified and set in the unchanging perceptual environment". This is but one of a number of recent studies which suggest that normal concentration, perception and thought can only be maintained in a constantly changing environment. Where, over a long period, there is no change, a condition described as "sensory deprivation" occurs, in which capacity to concentrate deteriorates and attention fluctuates and lapses. Therefore, if we feel a child must be protected from the stimulation of the classroom, it is important to realize that he cannot profitably tolerate this "sensory deprivation" for too long.

4. *Children with Disorders of Language Development*

Writing of children with disorders of language development, Morley (1957) estimated that at the age of 4 years, as many as 5 per cent of children may still have unintelligible speech and that many of these children later have reading difficulties. It has been demonstrated in nursery school units for children with delayed speech that many of these children can, with extra help given at an early age, catch up and take their place normally in school. Severe cases of developmental dysphasia, however, need very skilled and specialized teaching. These children are frequently diagnosed as mentally subnormal. Without speech and in the case of receptive aphasics, with very little comprehension of speech, it is often difficult to determine to what extent the child's language delay is due to mental retardation. While it is true that most mentally subnormal children are slower in language development than are normal children of the same age, careful observation of a non-speaking child, together with the use of non-verbal tests instructions for which can be demonstrated without speech can distinguish the child whose poor and delayed language development is due to overall mental subnormality from those normal or bright children whose speech handicap is specific. Confusion sometimes arises in distinguishing the aphasic from the autistic child. Autistic children truly fit the definition of "non-communicating", in the sense that their withdrawal from emotional relationships with people is gross and sustained. Consequently, speech is either lost or never acquired or when stereotyped words and phrases are spoken, they are not used as a means of ordinary communication. The emotional climate of the aphasic child is quite different, in that he is very much aware of and seeks normal emotional relationships with people. Where communication by speech is not adequate to convey meaning, gestures and mime are frequently used.

The problem of helping children with delayed language development during the pre-school years is very complicated, since the causes of the delay are not always clear. There are many children whose speech delay is related directly to poor opportunities at home. The effect of social differences in language development has been clearly demonstrated by Bernstein (1960) and others. These are the so-called "disadvantaged" children, for whom speech provision is being made extensively in the United States in their "Head start" programmes. It would be expected that, given more opportunities for play experiences and extended "language-oriented" programmes for pre-school children, these deprived children would show measurable improvement. Various approaches to language remediation programmes are discussed in such monographs as that edited by Brottman (1968), in which the merits of rigid programming, as against a freer approach, are demonstrated by results obtained.

In a discussion of the mental development of the 2-year old,

Bayley (1966) shows how between the years of 2 and 3 basic language, i.e. verbal communication and comprehension, is most crucial for mental growth. She quotes here a study in language stimulation that was undertaken in Sonoma State Hospital, where in July 1965 a group of mongoloid children underwent a period of intensive training, designed to increase their receptive and expressive language abilities. The study, described in some detail, demonstrates that if instituted at the right time, appropriate training can, within genetic or other biological limits, improve language functioning.

Many local education authorities in Great Britain have also set up units for pre-school children with delayed speech. There is, for example, in Bristol, a small unit for six to eight children with delayed speech, catered for within a normal nursery school.

More recently the Wolfson Centre (1973) has started an intervention programme for children with language delay. This is financed largely by a grant from the Department of Education and Science. This is a five-year project still only in its first year.

This kind of provision might help the children identified in the study group as having delayed language development. But where the damage at birth has been severe the child may, like Cedric, described earlier, need much more highly specialized help. However, the availability of this for pre-school children is limited by a shortage of trained speech therapists in this country. Where special nursery school provision is not available, it is important that the parent should have guidance and helpful direction in ways of initiating early training for the pre-school child. The problems of diagnosis of children with communication disorders are very complicated and differential diagnosis requires a highly skilled team of specialists.

Having identified those children whose deviant development alerts us to the possibility that they may have specific learning disorders when faced with formal schooling, an important next step should be careful diagnosis of the nature and character of their problems. Only on the basis of this can sound and helpful methods of teaching then be founded.

To date, there has been comparatively little reliably planned research into the best teaching methods for this group, the main criterion for success at present is that "it seems to work".

In the Plowden Report (1967) on children and their primary schools, there is a strong recommendation for a large expansion of nursery education in this country. All specialists whose work is with children—developmental paediatricians, psychologists, social workers, child-care officers and teachers—are consistently more aware of the importance of early identification and, if necessary, early treatment of children with specific difficulties. An extension of nursery school provision would make it more possible for these children to be detected early and ascertained in time for good treatment provision to be made available for them.

CHAPTER 5

Children in School

MANY of the observations made in the previous chapter regarding pre-school or nursery school age children remain relevant for children during the infant school period, which in English schools usually lasts from 5 to 7 or 8 years. For the teacher, the main indications that a child may need extra or different help lie in the development of language and in motor abilities. As the child progresses towards junior school age, i.e. 7 plus, more specific learning difficulties begin to become apparent.

By the age of 7 years, the teacher will probably have become very much aware of the child who is having difficulty in the beginnings of reading. It is very often the case that children who have been slow in acquiring language at 3 years show up again with reading difficulties in the beginnings of learning to read at the age of 6 to 7 years. There may also be children who, in spite of good language development, have had visuo-spatial perceptual difficulties which give rise to reading difficulties for them in the early school years.

Children noticed in pre-school and infant school years as "clumsy" children very often have great difficulty in managing writing and setting down figures and sums. These children also find difficulty not only in the recognition of, but also in copying letters and figures in correct orientation. The confusion of direction of letters lasts much longer for these children than for the normally developing young child.

In later school years, persistent difficulties in reading, poor spelling, slow and awkward writing, poorly developed concept of number, as well as difficulty in games and manipulative activities which require good motor co-ordination, should all be regarded as indications that the child is experiencing difficulties which might be accounted for by neurological handicap or severe maturational lags. If this is the case, a special approach to helping them in school work might be tried with benefit.

If the child is brought to notice by his teacher, the problem will first be considered by the school medical officer, who is then likely, depending on the kind of facilities available in the area, to refer the case either to the school psychological service or to a child guidance clinic directed by a psychiatrist.

As is only to be expected, these children will inevitably have reacted by behaviour disorders to emotional pressures arising from their difficulties. The detection of a specific learning disability may, therefore, easily be complicated by an overlay of psychosomatic and behaviour disorders. This emphasizes the need for true co-operation and communication between disciplines in order to arrive at a sound diagnosis and from that a useful plan for helping the child in school.

It is important that the child should be screened for all possible causes of poor achievement in school—social factors, which frequently influence the kind of opportunities and encouragements given at home, sporadic absences from school due to poor health, sensory deficits particularly of vision and hearing, neurological signs of dysfunction and also factors related to intellectual functioning.

The Psychologist's Contribution

Although this whole concept of the child with organic impairment remains still confused and uncertain in its boundaries, it is generally possible, by means of careful psychological diagnostic procedures, to lay down at least some guide-lines to help the teacher in his approach to the particular child's problem. The time has passed when the psychologist would use the diagnostic rag-bag of "brain-damaged" to cover all such a child's problems, sometimes throwing in for good measure, "he needs individual remedial teaching". Such a label could be both damaging and misleading. In the first place, the term "brain-damaged" is an alarming concept to many parents. In the second, the sense of irreversibility it conveys carries a feeling of hopelessness for teachers. These children vary so greatly that to group them all together as needing only extra and individual teaching, regardless of teaching method, is quite useless. While the value of individual help for children who are failing in school work, carrying with it, as is so often the case, a satisfying personal relationship, cannot be decried, children with specific learning disorders need a special approach to methods of learning.

These must be based on a careful diagnostic assessment of their individual difficulties. Otherwise children who have been given hope and encouragement when individual teaching has been provided may have their confidence in the possibility of succeeding completely destroyed.

This is because they have still made little or no progress with individual tuition, using the same unsuitable method already experienced in class.

The psychologist's tools for diagnostic assessment are as yet imprecise. Our knowledge of the whole field of learning difficulties due primarily to central nervous system damage or inherent deviant maturation is constantly being extended or modified by new research. Yet by a thoughtful use of the tools we have, and in collaboration with medical colleagues, it is possible for the psychologist to make sufficient differential in diagnosis to be able to give the teacher the underlying basic reasons for selecting a particular kind of teaching approach for a particular child.

When faced with a request for help for a child who is failing in certain specified school subjects, the psychologist will need as much information as possible and will usually have had a school report and also some background history from the parents. Paediatric and neurological examinations, together with careful investigation of the child's vision and hearing, will have been made at some point in the diagnostic procedure. The order in which this is carried out will depend on the channel through which the child has been referred for psychological diagnosis, but even if the paediatric and neurological examination has to follow, it is well to have a careful vetting of vision and hearing, if possible before the child is seen by the psychologist.

Assuming then that the child's discrepant functioning is not due to visual or hearing deficit, the obvious first task of the psychologist is to get some measure of his overall or global intellectual level, as far as this is possible, despite the unevenness of functioning.

Tests for Assessment of Level of Overall Intellectual Functioning

For young school children, the test which has the most general use is the 1960 L–M Revision of the Stanford-Binet Intelligence Scale. This test is very heavily biased towards measurement of mental abilities necessary for success in school subjects. Nevertheless, it provides a simple score, which gives some estimate of the child's general level of intellectual functioning at the time.

A more generally useful test for purposes of diagnosis in children presenting the kind of unevenness of functioning and difficulties such as is the concern here, is the Wechsler Intelligence Scale for Children. Although this test was standardized in the United States for children of an age range from 5 to 15 years, it has not been found very accurately discriminating in children below 7 years in this country. This test has now been very usefully supplemented by Wechsler (1967) in his downward extension of the W.I.S.C., namely the Wechsler Pre-School and Primary Scale of Intelligence for Children aged 4–6½ years (the W.P.P.S.I.).

An empirical evaluation of the W.P.P.S.I. with a British sample has been made by Yule *et al.* (1969). The test battery was tried out with 150 5-year-olds living on the Isle of Wight, in order to test the applicability of the scale with British children, and to try out certain substitutes for some obvious "Americanisms" contained in the scale.

On the evidence of this study as a whole, the W.P.P.S.I. was found to be a comparatively well standardized test. In interpreting results with British children, it is suggested that the expected mean on the Full-Scale I.Q. is about 105. Verbal–Performance discrepancies appear to be larger among British children and the reasons for these differences are discussed by Yule.

Like the W.I.S.C., this test consists of five sub-tests which combine to present a result in terms of a "Verbal I.Q." and five presented as a "Performance I.Q.". The total score—"Full Scale I.Q."—is a weighted combination of the scores from the whole scale. If the child's verbal score on the W.I.S.C. or the W.P.P.S.I. is significantly higher (twenty or more points) than the performance score and if the tasks which the child finds particularly difficult are those which involve visual-spatial ability, such as block design and object assembly, with also a very low score on the arithmetic and coding sub-tests, it suggests that the child has a specific visuo-spatial difficulty.

When a child makes a much higher score on the performance scale than on the verbal, the possibility of a language handicap and the reasons for it need further exploration. Since there is no single interpretation for any pattern of verbal–performance differences, any discrepancies in sub-test scores must be taken as a signal to the psychologist that further exploration is necessary. Although discrepancies such as those described above indicate the possibility that the learning disability for which a child has been referred may arise from neurological impairment or disorderly maturation, this diagnosis cannot be made on the findings of psychological assessments alone. Paediatric and neurological vetting is also essential. By careful diagnostic testing, however, the psychologist can make an important contribution to remedial teaching for the child concerned.

Having obtained an overall assessment of the child's present level of functioning, it is useful to make a formal assessment of his educational attainments, particularly in the subjects in which he is experiencing difficulty and in comparison with his attainments in other basic school subjects and also with his global I.Q. Clarke (1966) rightly regards the information gained by the procedures discussed above as descriptive rather than explanatory.

"Description," he says, "by itself is unlikely to identify the appropriate methods of treatment . . . although it lays the foundation for inquiring."

Tests which Reveal Intellectual Strengths and Weaknesses and Provide Guides to Appropriate Teaching Methods for Children with Varying Learning Difficulties

The value of tests which analyse attainments in specific areas of functioning has been demonstrated in the work of psychologists in the United States.

The two tests described below provide good examples of this kind of approach.

1. *Developmental Test of Visual Perception*

Working in Los Angeles with children who had severe learning disabilities, Frostig (1961) and her colleagues found that difficulties in visual perception created by far the major problems in learning for many of the children who had been diagnosed as having brain damage. They found that children who had difficulty in writing seemed to be handicapped in eye–hand co-ordination and children who could not recognize words often had disturbances in figure–ground perception. They also postulated that children who had difficulty in recognizing a letter when written in different sizes or colours had poor form constancy. Children who made reversals or rotations were having trouble in perceiving position in space, while interchanging the orders of letters indicated difficulties in analysing spatial relationships. On the basis of this, Frostig and her colleagues (1964) published a *Developmental Test of Visual Perception*. Norms were based on over 1800 children between ages 3 and 9 years. The test was designed to measure certain perceptual abilities which Frostig believes to develop relatively independently of each other. These areas of functioning were chosen because defects in these abilities were observed in work with children with learning difficulties.

Carefully graded tasks are presented as five sub-tests.

1. The first of these is eye-motor co-ordination. The child's task is to draw straight and curved lines between increasingly narrow boundaries. Examples of this are shown in Fig. 15.
2. In the second task, figure–ground perception, the child is asked to discriminate between intersecting figures (Fig. 16).
3. Perception of form constancy, in which the task is to detect squares and circles among other shapes on the page (Fig. 17).
4. Perception of position in space is tested by asking the child to detect a reversed or rotated figure in a sequence (Fig. 18).
5. Perception of spatial relations. The task here is to copy patterns by linking dots (Fig. 19).

In these five areas of visual perception, Frostig found evidence of age progression from 3 years to about $7\frac{1}{2}$. Studies of the Bender (1938) Gestalt test with children also show a steady improvement up to the age of about 8 years, during which time the Bender differentiates both outstanding and immature visual motor perception. After that, the test no longer discriminates at the upper ages. Evidence from both these types of test of visuo-motor perception would seem to bear out Piaget's thesis that from around the age of 7 to $7\frac{1}{2}$, cognitive functions begin to predominate and perceptuo-motor skills should already be established.

In Frostig's (1961) normative work with her test, she made a comparative study of 71 children who had been medically identified as "neurologically handicapped". She not only found that their total scores were lower than those of her normal group, but also the scatter of scores between the various sub-tests was much greater than that of the normal group. Frostig suggests that the test results of the "abnormal" group show that they suffered a maturational delay in development of visual perceptual ability. She also holds that the separate functions of visual perception tested can be disturbed independently. It is on this assumption that she bases her training programmes to meet the needs of individual children, since she holds that there is a specific relationship between the developmental level in these skills and the child's

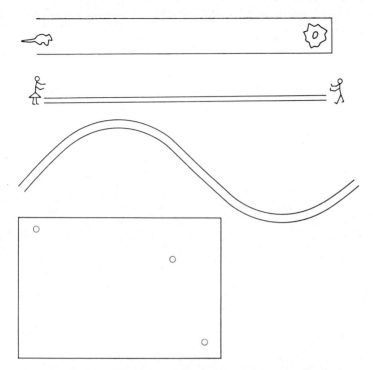

Fig. 15. Samples of items from sub-test 1 (eye-motor co-ordination). (By permission of Dr. Marianne Frostig and Consulting Psychologists Press.)

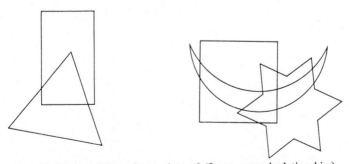

Fig. 16. Samples of items from sub-test 2 (figure–ground relationship.) (By permission of Dr. Marianne Frostig and Consulting Psychologists Press.)

111

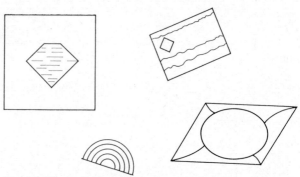

FIG. 17. Samples of items from sub-test 3 (constancy of form).
(By permission of Dr. Marianne Frostig and Consulting Psychologists
Press.)

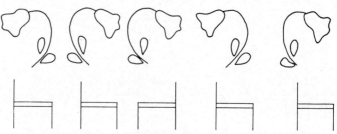

FIG. 18. Examples of items from sub-test 4 (position in space).
(By permission of Dr. Marianne Frostig and Consulting Psychologists
Press.)

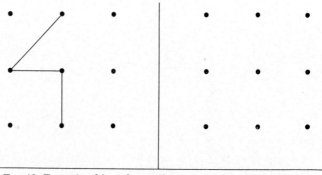

FIG. 19. Example of item from sub-test 5 (spatial relationships).
(By permission of Dr. Marianne Frostig and Consulting Psychologists
Press.)

ability to learn. This is her basis for using this test as a diagnostic tool. The test has not yet been widely used in this country. One or two research studies are in progress in England, mainly to assess the value of the teaching method constructed by Frostig on the findings of the test. This will be discussed in a later chapter. Much research remains to be done before the test can be accepted as reliably giving all that is claimed for it.

2. *Differential Diagnosis of Linguistic Ability*

A similar example of the construction of a test for purposes of differential diagnosis is the Illinois Test of Psycholinguistic Abilities by McCarthy and Kirk (1961). A revised standardised edition of this test was published in 1970. This test is an attempt to measure various aspects of language development in children and is based on Osgood's theory of language acquisition and use. This involves two channels of communication: (1) auditory and visual inputs, and (2) vocal and motor outputs. It involves two levels of organization—a representational or meaning level and an automatic sequential level. There are also three processes: decoding, association and encoding. It is presented in a series of nine sub-tests, which it is believed cover the range of "psycholinguistic" abilities.

First, there are six tests at a representational level. These all assess some aspect of the child's ability to deal with meaningful symbols. They are divided into "decoding" tests, "visual decoding", by which is meant the ability to comprehend the meaning of pictures and printed words, "auditory decoding" which is the ability to comprehend the spoken word, and "association tests" which assess the ability to relate meaning to visual or auditory symbols. The latter are "visual-motor association" tests, in which the child's ability to relate meaningful visual symbols is assessed by such tasks as selecting from a number of pictures the one which most meaningfully relates to a given stimulus picture. The two easiest and two most difficult of the series are shown in Figs. 20–25. Similarly, there is an auditory–vocal association test, which measures the child's ability to relate spoken words in a

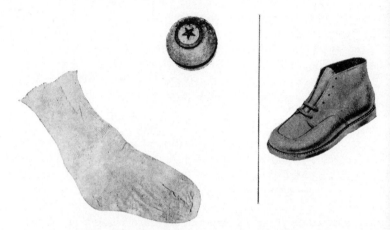

FIG. 20. (*The Illinois Test of Psycholinguistic Abilities*, Experimental Edition, James J. McCarthy and Samuel A. Kirk, University of Illinois.)

FIG. 21. (*The Illinois Test of Psycholinguistic Abilities*, Experimental Edition, James J. McCarthy and Samuel A. Kirk, University of Illinois.)

Fig. 22. (*The Illinois Test of Psycholinguistic Abilities*, Experimental Edition, James J. McCarthy and Samuel A. Kirk, University of Illinois.)

meaningful way. This ability is tested, as it is in many intelligence tests, by analogies. These begin with "I sit on a chair; I sleep on a ...", and through 26 questions, graded in difficulty, reach "An ocean is deep; a pond is ...".

The final series in the representational level are "encoding" tests, by which the ability to put ideas into words or gestures is assessed. Under this heading, there are vocal and motor encoding tests. The vocal ones require description of simple objects and the motor ones assess ability to express ideas by gestures or mime.

In this series, the tests are at the representational level. The last three sub-tests are designated as being at the "automatic–sequential level". They are measures of long-term retention or short-term memory of symbol sequences, not necessarily meaningful ones. The purpose of the first test, described as "auditory–vocal automatic test" is said to be to "sample the subject's repertoire of grammatical rules". The responses are described as "automatic". They are said to "permit one to give conscious attention to the content of a message while the words with which to express that message seem to come automatically". This is a

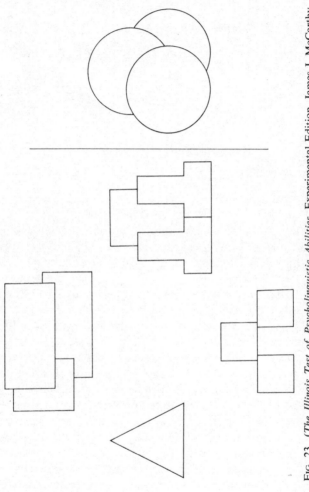

Fig. 23. (*The Illinois Test of Psycholinguistic Abilities*, Experimental Edition, James J. McCarthy and Samuel A. Kirk, University of Illinois.)

sentence completion technique in which pictures are used. For example card 1 (see Fig. 24). "Here [point] is an apple. Here [point] are two . . . ." These take the child through basic grammatical structures to the most difficult of the series (see

FIG. 24. (*The Illinois Test of Psycholinguistic Abilities*, Experimental Edition, James J. McCarthy and Samuel A. Kirk, University of Illinois.)

FIG. 25. (*The Illinois Test of Psycholinguistic Abilities*, Experimental Edition, James J. McCarthy and Samuel A. Kirk, University of Illinois.)

Fig. 25). "The thief is stealing the jewels. These are the jewels he . . . ."

The last two sub-tests are "sequencing tests," in which is assessed the ability to reproduce a sequence of symbols correctly by means of visual or auditory memory. They are tests of auditory–vocal sequencing, which is assessed by a form of digit repetition test and a test of visual-motor sequencing, in which the child is required to duplicate the order of a sequence of pictures or geometric designs shown to the child and then removed.

The Frostig developmental test of visual perception and McCarthy and Kirk's test of psycholinguistic abilities have been described in some detail because they illustrate the present American approach to differential diagnosis of children with specific learning disabilities. The Wepman (1958) Test of Auditory Discrimination is also frequently used in American schools, though it is generally held in Great Britain that doubts about a child's auditory discrimination are best resolved by a careful test of hearing, carried out by a skilled otologist. The way in which the findings of such tests are used as an aid to planning suitable remedial teaching programmes will be discussed later.

British psychologists await with interest the completion of a new intelligence scale, devised and standardized in Britain. The construction of this scale is financed by a research grant from the Department of Education and Science and was initiated by the British Psychological Society, which set up a Consultative Committee under the directorship of the late Professor Warburton of Manchester University.

It is planned that this scale will eventually cover the age-range from 2 to 18 years and it will be constructed in the form of sub-scales, which cover specialized abilities. While the final shape of the test is by no means decided, sub-scales which assess the following specialized abilities are being tried out: (1) Reasoning, (2) Verbal, (3) Spatial, (4) Number, (5) Memory and (6) Fluency.

Combined scores from the whole test will provide an index of general mental ability. But it is hoped to construct longer forms of some of the sub-scales, to enable psychologists to make a more thorough investigation of individual cases, where the need for diagnosis of special problems arises.

The test draws heavily on the work of Piaget on the development of children's thinking and it will be possible to obtain scores showing the qualitative level of thinking attained, for example, pre-logical, concrete and propositional.

It is hoped, therefore, that with the introduction of this test, standardized on British children, it will be possible to identify a child's strengths and weaknesses in cognitive functioning by the use of a tool more integrated for this purpose than any at present available in this country.

It is only out of a proper diagnosis of assets and deficits that a suitable treatment programme can be planned. Examples of the value and also the limitations in the use of diagnostic psychological tests are seen in the presentation of the four cases which follow.

Case Histories of Children Referred on Account of Reading Disabilities

The four cases described here are chosen to illustrate the kind of differential diagnosis that is possible, using the psychological tools of assessment at present available.

Much of the diagnostic work, as well as the choice of a remedial teaching programme is largely influenced by the character of the educational system of the country to which it belongs and the kind of special provision available for children with special difficulties. To illustrate this with reference to British children, four cases have been chosen as examples of the different categories described earlier and with which we are concerned in this book. The children were all 7 or 8 years old when they were referred to a hospital clinic. This, in terms of the English educational system, means that they had reached the end of their time in the infants' school and were about to go, or had already just been moved into the junior school. They were all referred primarily because they had serious reading difficulties. It is generally a reason for concern if a child reaches this point of change in the primary school without having mastered the beginnings of reading. Teachers in the junior part of the school are not always as well equipped by training for teaching the beginnings of reading as are the infants' teachers, nor is there usually so much opportunity for individually helping a child who is falling behind his group. It is not surprising, therefore, that many referrals for reading difficulty should occur at

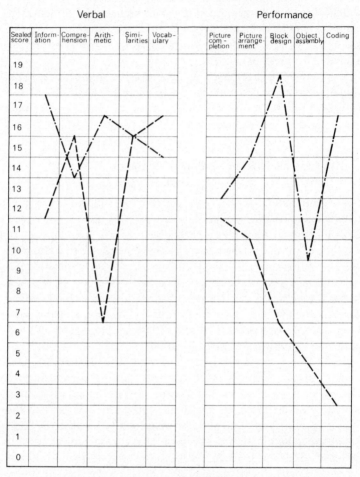

Fig. 26. Scaled scores on the W.I.S.C.

about the age of moving from infants to junior sections of the primary school. It will be seen how the diagnostic investigation of these four children demonstrated the need for a quite different approach to remedial teaching for each of the four children.

Case 1. Donald B. (aged 8 years). This boy had been examined by the school medical officer, at the request of his school teacher, because of his extreme difficulty with reading, writing, copying and number. At the time, he was attending a small primary school and had reached the age when he had to move into the junior section of the school. This was a small, village-type primary school. It was not streamed, so that the forty children of junior school age were under the care of one teacher. Both Donald's class teacher and the head teacher were greatly puzzled by Donald and quite at a loss to know how best to help him. Although Donald was a delicate looking child, wearing very thick glasses, on medical examination his vision, corrected by glasses, was normal and he had no hearing loss. When he came for psychological assessment, the school teacher sent a very thoughtful report, in which she said he had made no beginning in reading and had no concept of number. He was clumsy and awkward in motor manipulation, both fine and gross. He could not write, nor could he even copy the initials of his own name, clearly printed— D.B. They said also that his span of concentration was extremely short and he very quickly became fatigued. In spite of all this his teacher was puzzled because she wrote, "on occasions his memory and power of thought is outstanding". She also remarked on his poor manual ability, his difficulty in putting on his coat and tying his shoe-laces and his quick and almost uncontrollable reaction to frustration when faced with a task he could not manage to do. She described his speech as being, in times of stress, almost unintelligible. Yet, despite all his defects, she resisted the suggestion that he was probably a mentally sub-normal child of low overall I.Q. And she was genuinely seeking advice on ways of helping him.

Donald was a small, restless boy and it was difficult to hold his attention for long at a time. Tested on the Wechsler Intelligence Scale for Children, his Verbal I.Q. was 114, Performance

I.Q. was 76 and Full Scale I.Q. was 96. Sub-test scores on the graph (Fig. 26) show the very marked unevenness in his abilities. The only score on the Verbal Scale which falls below average is

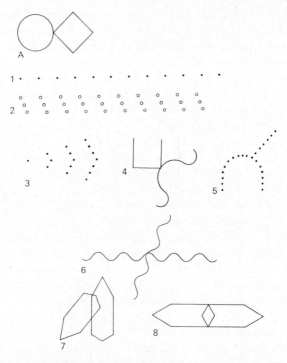

FIG. 27. Bender designs for the Visual Motor Gestalt Test. (*A Visual Motor Gestalt Test and Its Clinical Use*, Dr. Lauretta Bender, Copyright, the American Orthopsychiatric Association, Inc. Reproduced with permission.)

arithmetic, but all the tasks which draw on visuo-spatial ability are very low indeed.

Educational attainments in the basic subjects were virtually nil.

Although Donald's articulation was poor, his use and comprehension of language was well above average for his age.

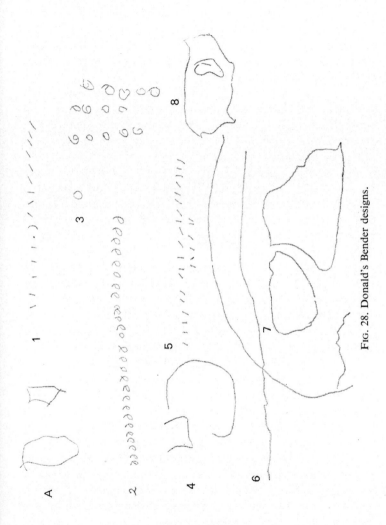

FIG. 28. Donald's Bender designs.

On the Bender Visual Motor Gestalt test, he not only made a very poor score, but his drawings all showed the kind of characteristics found, according to Koppitz's (1964) study of the test with children, only in brain-injured children after the age of $6\frac{1}{2}$–7 years. A comparison with the designs on Fig. 27 and those of Donald on Fig. 28 show the distortions and failure to integrate, so characteristic of certain brain-injured children.

Without going too deeply into the scoring of Donald's test performance, his drawings show many of the deviations from the copy, that Koppitz in her research studies found significant of children with organic involvement. Examples of these are Donald's difficulty in integrating parts seen in his reproductions in Fig. 28 of designs A,5, 4 and 8 and in 2 where he omits two rows of circles, the basic configuration or design distortion seen in designs A,5, 7 and 8; straight lines for curves as in 7; substitution of circles and loops for dots as in 3 or substitution of lines for dots, as in 1 and 5; disproportion and missing angles, as on the hexagons in 8.

Donald also had poor left–right discrimination and his self-portrait (Fig. 29) had all the vagueness and confusion seen in the self-portaits of much younger cerebral palsied children.

The following history was given by his mother.

Donald, an only child, was born normally in hospital. His birth weight was 7 lb 7 oz. He was circumcized at 1 week and had tongue-tie which was dealt with. He had great feeding difficulty and at 10 weeks was transferred to a London teaching hospital. A meningeal infection was treated with streptomycin. Donald stayed in this hospital for one month and was then moved to their convalescent home in the country. He was discharged after 5 months and came to his own home for the first time at 6 months. His developmental progress was slow. He sat up at 11 months and walked at 20 months. His articulation was poor and his poor sight had to be corrected with glasses from infancy. As an only child who had suffered such severe illness as a baby, involving as it did early and prolonged separation, it is understandable that the parents protected him anxiously. He was always a restless, hyperkinetic child and it can readily be understood how his restless behaviour and school difficulties could be interpreted as the difficult behaviour of an emotionally maladjusted, over-protected child. Careful examination of his response to the diagnostic psychological assessments, together with the sensitive

FIG. 29. Donald's self-portrait.

report from the school, however, presents this boy as an almost classic example of what could be described as "the Strauss syndrome".

Although Donald was referred primarily for advice regarding his difficulty in learning to read, his learning problems are embedded in his total behavioural response to his world. To have any success, a remedial teaching programme would have to be carried out within a setting that could cater suitably for him wholly, recognizing his perceptual, motor and behavioural problems as part of a total syndrome.

Compare this with:

Case 2. Joe M. (aged 7 years). This boy was also referred as a child who had not made a start in reading. The urge for further investigation came from the parents, but Joe's teacher agreed that it was "a little worrying" that such an obviously bright child was having such difficulty.

This boy was tested on the W.I.S.C. He is an intelligent boy—Verbal I.Q. 131, Performance I.Q. 127—Full Scale I.Q. 132. Subtest scores are shown in Fig. 26, page 120. Although his Performance I.Q. is above average, it is considerably lower than his Verbal I.Q., in spite of the fact that his highest score on the whole test was in block design. His performance score was mainly lowered by his poorer achievement on object assembly. Joe's poor performance on the object assembly test suggests some difficulty in visuo-spatial perception, but not so severe as to account for his reading difficulty. His competence in doing the block design test was quite remarkable. Joe's execution of the Bender Gestalt test was well up to his age-level (Fig. 30)—7 years. He had some difficulty in drawing a self-portrait (Fig. 31), but its clarity of conception contrasts markedly with that of Donald, who was a year older.

Tested on the Neale Analysis of Reading Ability, Joe's reading accuracy age was 5 years, 10 months, but his level of comprehension was at age 8 years, 5 months.

A history was given by the mother. Joe is the oldest of four children. Next in the family is a brother, who is 18 months younger. There are two younger sisters. Joe's birth weight was 10 lb 10 oz. He was born after a long labour, but the delivery was normal. During birth, his heart stopped, he had to be resuscitated and it

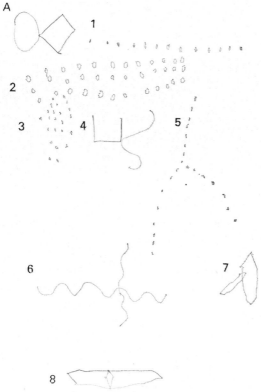

FIG. 30. Joe's Bender designs.

was thought possible that slight perinatal anoxia would result. Joe crawled at 1 year and walked at 17 months. His mother could not remember when he began to talk, but had an impression that his speech was later than that of the younger children. At 18 months, Joe had to be in hospital for a few days. While he was

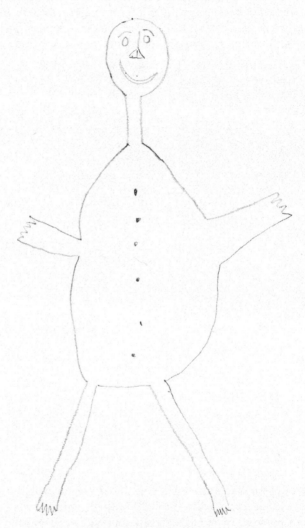

FIG. 31. Joe's self-portrait.

there, the nurse expressed surprise that he could not feed himself with a spoon. This was the first indication that the family had of any motor disability. Joe is now a noticeably clumsy child. He is still awkward with a knife and fork and tries to avoid using them. It is for this reason that he hates school dinners. He tends to knock things over and he cannot run as fast as his younger brother. He is slow to fasten buttons and cannot tie shoe laces. He gets teased when he cannot keep up with the other children at play.

Joe's vision and hearing are normal. Although he has very good language comprehension and usage, his articulation is very poor. When talking freely or in moments of excitement or frustration, he finds it very difficult to get words out. He still has many consonant substitutions. The neurological examination revealed a mild left hemiparesis.

This boy is one of the group of "clumsy" children. His motor disability is most evident in his speech and he would fall into the category of children described by Brain (1961) as suffering from "developmental articulatory dyspraxia". Although he has difficulty in making the movements required for tying up shoe laces and buttoning, his visuo-spatial ability is within the range of normal development. His reading difficulty would seem to be directly related to his poor articulation and a remedial reading programme should be linked with speech therapy, in which good phonetic training in sounds of words should play a major part.

The most suitable kind of approach to teaching this boy, therefore, would be very different from that necessary to help Donald (case 1), though both these children's difficulties would seem to arise from minor damage at birth, or in the neo-natal period.

Cases 3 and 4, also referred at 7 and 8 years of age on account of difficulty in learning to read, are children who would fall into the second major category, described as children with language handicaps.

Case 3. Ronald F. (aged 8 years). This boy was already well settled in the junior section of his primary school. The school had asked for help because they had rightly judged him to be an exceptionally bright child, but said that his reading was poor and he seemed to have great difficulty in grasping the meaning of material presented orally. There was some doubt in the minds of Ronald's teachers about his hearing. This boy did not begin to speak until he was $3\frac{1}{2}$ and, on the recommendation of a paediatrician, to whom the parents had gone for advice, he had attended a nursery school for deaf and aphasic children. At 5 years, however, he had a very careful examination by an otologist, who said that he had no hearing loss and that he needed the stimulation of a community of normally speaking children. He started formal schooling, therefore, in a small primary school where he gradually developed more and more speech, though his teachers always felt that there was something a little odd about him.

Ronald was the oldest of three children. The parents were both professional people. Ronald's birth was normal. He weighed $8\frac{1}{2}$ lb at birth and he developed normally, except for speech. He only began to say recognizable single words at $3\frac{1}{2}$ years and did not speak in small sentences until after 4 years. As part of this diagnostic investigation, he was tested very carefully by Dr. Mary Sheridan (1968) for vision and hearing, using her own Stycar Tests (1958). He showed normal distant and also close vision. The following is taken from her report on this boy:

"*Hearing*. The pure tone audiogram showed good hearing over the whole speech range, including the high frequencies." Of his hearing she reported:

> Hearing for single consonants, slowly delivered up to ten feet and for single words as tested in quiet, conversational voice at ten feet, with Stycar high-frequency word list slowly delivered, was normal. When, however, he was asked to repeat at ten feet sentences spoken at ordinary conversational level and rate, a task which is usually well within the capacity of five- to seven-year-old children, he immediately began to falter, repeating the first word or two and then becoming lost. This type of response usually indicates some delay in auditory perception, quite independent of both auditory acuity and willingness to listen.
>
> *Comment*. Ronald's visual and auditory acuity are normal, but he has difficulty in auditory perception. This perceptual anomaly was probably responsible for his original delay in speaking and his present problems of recall, particularly in reading and spelling.
>
> The aetiology of these conditions is obscure, although it is generally

accepted by developmental paediatricians that they have neurological associations and tend to run in families and indicate some delay in structure or functional maturation of the central nervous system.

I have quoted rather fully from this report as it illustrates so well the value of co-operation between disciplines in reaching a diagnostic goal.

Tested on the W.I.S.C., his Verbal I.Q. was 121, his Performance I.Q. was 124 and Full Scale I.Q. 125. The pattern of his sub-test scores shown in Fig. 32 is very even.

On the Neale Analysis of Reading Ability, his reading accuracy age was 7 years and his age for reading for comprehension was 6 years, 11 months. His spelling age on Schonell's Graded Word Spelling Test was 6 years, 4 months. His mental age was nearer ten years.

Ronald's late speaking and apparent inability, in spite of normal hearing, to discriminate and hence appreciate the significance of sounds did not at first unduly worry his parents, since on his mother's side there was a clear family history of his condition. Ronald's delayed speech, despite normal hearing, would seem to be an hereditary auditory imperception, related to disorderly maturation rather than to any cerebral impairment. It would seem that Ronald's two younger brothers will have similar difficulty. Ronald's parents adopted a baby girl and they described their delight at having a baby who "babbles" and how vividly this baby was making them realize what a silent family their own had been.

Ronald is an intelligent boy and although his achievement is not what would be expected from a boy of his capacity, he is managing in a normal school. It was difficult at first for his teacher to understand his problem. He asked, "If as you say the boy is intelligent, why is he so slow to understand what is said to him?" Having, however, accepted that this is a problem for Ronald arising out of an inherent condition, he has exercised his ingenuity in seeking ways to broaden and increase Ronald's interest in an understanding of language usage.

Case 4. Michael H. (aged 7 years, 1 month). This boy was first

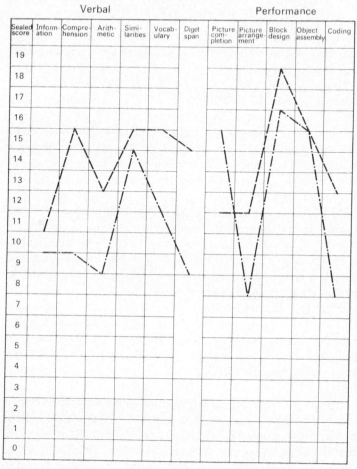

Case 3 – Ronald = — — — —

Case 4 – Michael = —·—·—·—·

FIG. 32. Scaled scores on the W.I.S.C.

referred at this age because after 2 years at school, he had made no beginning in reading. The parents had already expressed considerable anxiety about his school failure. Michael had attended a nursery school from $3\frac{1}{2}$ to 5 years of age. There, they had remarked on his lack of imaginative and make-believe play and his difficulty in getting meaning out of pictures or stories and in remembering them from one day to the next. It would seem that his development of inner language was slow and he was already showing difficulty in understanding the use of symbols. If we hold with Myklebust that reading is an integral part of symbolic behaviour, Michael's early behaviour at nursery school age suggests that he had a basic impairment in developing the use of symbolic language.

On formal testing with the W.I.S.C., Michael had a Verbal I.Q. of 99, Performance I.Q. 121 and Full Scale I.Q. 110. His sub-test scatter is interesting (see Fig. 32). His highest scores were on block design, object assembly and picture completion.

Michael's educational attainments were poor. He was a complete non-reader and his concept of number was barely at a 6-year level.

For further explanation of his reading difficulty, Frostig's Developmental Test of Visual Perception was given. Michael showed an even achievement on all the five sub-tests and his perceptual quotient was 116. His difficulty was not accounted for by poor development of visuo-spatial ability. On the Graham and Kendall Memory for Designs Test, given as a memory test, Michael did very badly, though when he was tried with the same test as a test of copying designs, his achievement was unusually good. Although he is right handed, when trying to copy the drawings with special care, he used his left hand. From his extensive experience in this field of study, Zangwill (1960 and 1962) stresses the importance of poorly developed laterality as a factor in dyslexia.

Michael was then given the Illinois Psycholinguistics Test. The profile of his results is shown in Fig. 33. The striking thing about this test was his very great difficulty in tests involving sequences.

Looking back to his W.I.S.C. scores, the same pattern emerges. His lowest scores are on picture arrangement and digit span.

All these factors are pointers to the possibility of a true developmental dyslexia.

Michael is an only son. He has one younger sister. There is a history of reading difficulty going back for certainly three generations in the family. There is also a history of poorly defined hand

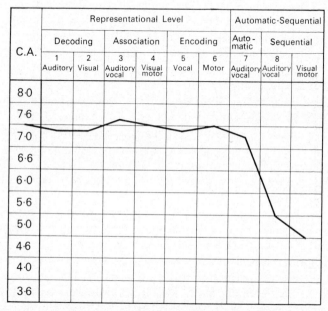

FIG. 33. Psycholinguistic profile—Michael, Case 4.

dominance in this family. Writing of *Cerebral Dominance and Its Relation to Psychological Function*, Zangwill (1960) puts forward the suggestion that "in the ambilateral the proper development of reading and writing, spatial judgement and directional control is relatively easily disturbed".

From the psychological diagnostic assessment, there were many indications that this boy's difficulties arose from a developmental dyslexia and suggestions for an approach to teaching were made on this assumption.

Although the referrals of these four children arose primarily from the fact that they were falling behind in school work, mainly in reading and allied subjects, it will be clear from the case histories that the kind of remedial programme most likely to help each of them differed widely from child to child. Since there are not as yet in this country any classes or units within the state school system geared specifically to children with learning difficulties arising from possible organic impairment, or from genetic conditions giving rise to disorders of maturation, provision for helping such children must be found within what is available and possible.

Let us look first at Donald (case 1), who has many problems. There is evidence in his discrepant psychological test scores of quite severe perceptual disorders. He always showed good facility in language, despite the fact that his articulation was poor, but he had great difficulty in doing tests that draw on visuo-motor and perceptual ability. He was a very clumsy child. This was seen in his difficulty in games, e.g. running, catching balls, as well as any task requiring controlled fine motor co-ordination. He could not easily find the way to put on his coat, nor, having managed that, could he do up the buttons or tie his shoe laces. Using a knife and fork presented him with an almost insuperable problem. He had great difficulty in copying and even recognizing and matching shapes and structures. Donald's learning problems were also greatly complicated by his excessive distractibility and his low frustration tolerance. Quite clearly, it was useless to suppose that he could lay down any firm foundation of learning in an unstreamed class of forty children, almost all of whom were above average in intelligence and ranged in age from 7 to 11 years. Donald needed a school environment where the class was small, and the external stimuli could be reduced to a minimum for the periods when he was engaged in learning the foundation work of the basic subjects. It was desirable, also, that he should be taught by someone who understood the problems of a child with

Donald's perceptual disabilities. But it was equally important that his specific learning disabilities should not be attacked separately, but as part of the deviations from normal behaviour which could only be understood in terms of damage which affected the whole organism. In many ways, it would have been easier to find suitable educational provision for Donald if he had been more severely physically handicapped and not just a "clumsy" child, because he had so many of the specific learning disabilities with which the teachers in our schools for cerebral palsied children are so well equipped to deal. He was, however, fortunate in that a very small class in the local authority area in which he lived had been set up to help children who were falling behind in school work and there was available to this small unit the advice of an educational psychologist, who had had considerable experience as an adviser to the schools organized by the Spastics' Society in this country.

During the period of junior school education, while Donald remained in this small remedial class, he made satisfactory progress, although it was slow. He always retained only a frail hold on what he had learned and in moments of extra anxiety or stress, he would lose it all and regress again to the younger child who had been so confused in orientation, completely "lost" in the difficulties involved in doing up his buttons and tying his shoe laces. At times like that, he could not read or write even his name. Just as he reached senior school age, unfortunately for Donald, the family moved into a different local education authority area and the only school available to him was a large secondary modern school. In spite of the fact that many contacts were made with the school and much explanation was given regarding his problems and needs, they were not able to give him the sort of protection and help he so badly needed. In an orderly and simple routine, the meaning and arrangement of which he could readily comprehend and give his mind to a clearly structured learning programme, in which he was not left to make choices and decisions for himself, Donald could manage. Without this, he quickly became lost in a large class of under-achievers.

This was a very severely damaged child, but one cannot help asking the question—could he have been helped to become more permanently stable and competent if the causes and nature of his learning problems had been diagnosed and treated earlier?

In case 2, Joe's problem was not so severe. He was a very intelligent child and when the reasons for his late reading and his emotional outbursts on meeting frustration in achievement or when being mocked and teased by his school mates for his poor success in games and sport (running and jumping) were clarified for his teachers, they were very sure that they could offer adequate remedial help within the school. A programme was arranged in which speech therapy was closely linked with a phonetic approach to extra help with reading. The parents also were greatly helped by having been given some extra insight into Joe's problems. For him, the most important need was to help him to articulate more clearly and to relate sounds to the symbols of letters and words. At the same time, a recognition of his motor handicap made it possible to allow concessions for his clumsiness and to protect him as far as possible from the frustrations that arose from being put in a situation outside his competence, that made him feel inferior and foolish in comparison with his peers. He was bright enough to accept help in gaining insight into his own limitations and to find ways of compensating for them.

This boy had many advantages. First, he was himself an intelligent boy and had the support of intelligent and understanding parents. He was fortunate also in having the help of an exceptionally competent and flexibly minded remedial teacher, who was able to work closely with a speech therapist, equally competent and flexible in her approach to remedial work. Consequently, Joe responded very quickly to this kind of approach to his reading difficulty. And as his reading improved, he quickly found real pleasure in reading for its own sake, in a home where books were plentifully available. His increased confidence and assurance had a marked effect on his total attitude to school life generally but he continues to react more sharply to frustrations and is more quickly confused than a normal undamaged child.

The children described here as cases 1 and 2 could both be classified as children whose learning difficulties arose primarily from neurological impairment of differing degrees of severity. They are examples of the categories 1a and 1b, as defined in Chapter 1.

The difference between these two children was very striking indeed and emphasizes the importance of treating each child as a unique individual, varying from others not only in the severity of the damage he has suffered, but also in his personality and his ways of adjusting to the difficulties of his life.

There are, however, certain characteristic difficulties arising from organic neurological impairment which occur fairly frequently in many of these children. Teaching help and, indeed, parental care becomes easier and more successful for the child if this is recognized and understood. They have been described by the present author in their relevance to children with cerebral palsy (1958, 1964 and 1965).

Cases 3 and 4 present quite different teaching problems. Both these boys, Ronald F. and Michael H., are children with language handicaps. They represent groups 2a and b respectively of the categories described in Chapter 1.

Discussing disorders of speech in childhood, Worster-Drought (1965) distinguishes between two kinds of disordered comprehension and reception of language. (1) Auditory aphasia, which he describes as "the inability to understand spoken language although hearing itself is intact". (2) Visual aphasia—"the inability to appreciate written or printed language although sight is normal."

Ronald's difficulties arise from the first of these. This has sometimes been called "word-deafness" or "central deafness", though these terms are misleading. Writing of this, Worster-Drought says, "The designation 'word-deafness' is too limited in scope to apply to this condition; moreover hearing loss as such plays no part in many of the cases and very little, if any, in other cases, spoken language being heard but not understood". He therefore suggested the term "congenital auditory imperception" as describing more completely the fundamental defect and he suggests that the pathological basis probably consists in an incomplete development of the auditory word-areas in the temporal lobe of the brain. This distinction was originally postulated by Wernicke in 1881.

It is possible that if Ronald's problem had been recognized in early childhood, without waiting for it to be highlighted by his under-achievement at school, Ronald might have been helped by more intensive training in the use of the tools of communication and the understanding and use of language.

Michael H. falls into the second of Worster-Drought's classifications. His reading difficulty is very severe indeed. Only long and patient teaching, using methods found to be appropriate for children with developmental dyslexia, could help this boy.

A large proportion of the children whose reading disability is diagnosed as developmental dyslexia have a history of late language development. Unlike the children who are thought to have organic neurological impairment, these dyslexics do not show the disordered perceptual development which creates such severe learning difficulties for the minimally brain-damaged child. True specific dyslexia occurs mostly in males and would appear to be genetically determined in about 90 per cent of cases. Like Michael, these children have great difficulty in sequential analysis and memorizing sequences, whether visual or auditory. Language is organized in a time–space pattern and speech, which demands sequential organization of linguistic units in time, is closely linked to reading. Poor auditory memory span and difficulties with analysis of auditory sequences create difficulties in reading and spelling. Reading also requires a successful response to the visual forms of language and it requires that the child not only sees the letters, but also grasps their symbolic significance. Many dyslexics have an undefined cerebral dominance and failure to develop a clear hand dominance usually results in difficulty with consistent left-to-right motor and perceptual organization, which is essential for reading, writing and spelling. Zangwill (1960) postulates a constitutionally determined maturational weakness in children whose hand dominance remains undefined. He suggests that the possessors of this type of cerebral organization are particularly vulnerable to the effects of stress and that in them the proper development of reading and writing, as well as spatial judgement and directional control, is easily disturbed by accidents of circumstance, among which he includes minimal brain injury at birth, predisposition to epilepsy, the after-effects of childish illness or even problems in psychological adjustment at home or at school.

The child whose reading disability is due to a specific developmental dyslexia can learn most readily through the phonetic method. Letters and sounds are the first important elements with which to begin. An alphabet tray, divided into small compartments, one for every letter of the alphabet, each of which contains several letters, is found to be a very helpful way for the severe dyslexic to learn. He begins by choosing letters from the tray to build up words and, later, short sentences. This sounding, choosing and actually manipulating the letters to form words, before reading and checking the accuracy of what he has produced, was found by workers in the Word Blind Centre in Copenhagen to be the most helpful approach to teaching so-called "word-blind" children to read. This is described briefly by Arkell (1966) and it illustrates a very different kind of teaching approach from that which would be most appropriate for a child whose neurological impairment complicates learning by reason of disorders of perception.

Although Michael has had very intensive coaching, using what are thought up to the present time to be the best methods for attacking this severe reading disability, his progress in reading remains limited. I do not think he will ever read for pleasure and reading will always be a difficult and burdensome task to him.

In his description of organic neurological factors related to learning disorders, Paine (1965) says, "It is probable that a child with the irregularities of cerebral function already described will find the process of growing up more traumatic than the majority of his age-mates. He perceives his environment somewhat different-ly, deals with sensory input in a somewhat different fashion and finally has difficulties in abstraction and conceptualisation, that is to say, in processes of internal thought". He goes on to point out that because these children are not so clearly different from the general population as are children with obvious physical handicaps, children with cerebral palsy, or even children with severe mental retardation, their difficulties tend to go unrecognized and they do not get the protection from pressures with which the obviously handicapped child is treated.

It is not surprising, therefore, that many of these children develop emotional disorders, which complicate their lives still further.

Although in discussing these four cases nothing has been said about emotional factors, such factors undoubtedly complicated diagnosis and treatment in all of them.

Following careful psychological testing and educational advice and arrangements, all these four children continued to be catered for within the normal school system. It is possible that had more specialized teaching units been available for case 1 (Donald) and case 4 (Michael), their progress would have been speedier and more successful. Had their condition been detected earlier, much emotional stress for themselves and their families could have been avoided.

There are many children, however, whose condition and consequent learning problems are much more intractable. The need for special educational provision for them is more urgent. Recent experiments in providing suitable education for these children are described in Chapter 6.

CHAPTER 6

Experiments in Teaching
Children with Specific Learning Difficulties

WRITING in Phase One of the project on Minimal Brain Dysfunction in Children, described in my Historical Survey Clements says:

> Within our limited validated knowledge concerning relationships between brain and behaviour, we must accept certain categories of deviant behaviour, developmental dyscrasias, learning disabilities and visual-motor-perceptual irregularities as valid indices of brain dysfunctioning. They represent neurological signs of a most meaningful kind and reflect disorganized central nervous system functioning at the highest level. To consider learning and behaviour as distinct and separate from other neurologic functions echoes a limited concept of the nervous system and of its various levels of influence and integration. We cannot afford the luxury of waiting until causes can be unquestionably established by techniques yet to be developed. We cannot postpone managing as effectively and honestly as' possible the large numbers of children who present chronic differences we feel are more related to organicity variables than others.

Influenced by a sense of the urgency of these children's needs, various pilot studies and experimental schools have been developed in the United States.

In 1961 Cruickshank and colleagues published an account of a demonstration-pilot study, which had been carried out with the purpose of assessing the value of a teaching method for hyperactive, emotionally disturbed children with and without clinically diagnosed brain-injury. Their two main aims in setting up this research study were: (1) to investigate and assess the usefulness of teaching methods developed in an experimental setting for brain-injured children and to evaluate their appropriateness to the instructional and social needs of hyperactive

142

and emotionally disturbed children, not showing evidence of brain injury, and (2) to carry out the pilot study within the framework of the administrative policies and procedures of a public school system.

The study was conducted within the public school system of Montgomery County, Maryland, and was housed in four classrooms in three elementary schools; two classes composed the experimental group and two the control group.

Forty children were selected whose emotional difficulties were characterized by hyperactive, aggressive behaviour and who were educationally retarded. They were between the chronological ages of 6 years 11 months and 10 years 11 months and they had mental ages of not less than 4 years 8 months and I.Q.s not less than 50. They were referred to the research team through the Montgomery County Public School Department of Special Education. Each child had an electro-encephalograph, paediatric, neurological, psychiatric, psychological and educational assessment and they were also examined for speech and hearing. Developmental and environmental data were also obtained. On the basis of all this information, the children were separated into two diagnostic groups:

1. Those children with clinically diagnosed neurological and medical evidence of brain injury.
2. Those children whose case histories showed psychological behaviour and learning disabilities similar to those observed in the brain-injured children, but whose diagnostic studies showed no conclusive evidence of specific birth injury, neurological signs or evidence of accident, disease or injury which might account for their behaviour and learning disorders.

The forty children were then placed in four matched groups of ten each. Five in each group of ten had a diagnostic classification of brain injury and the other five had a diagnostic classification of emotional disturbance. The four groups were matched also in terms of chronological age, mental age, level of educational attainment, degree of hyperactivity and perseveration and previous experience in special classes. Two of the four groups were treated as experimental groups and two as controls.

The two experimental groups were located in one school and the control groups were located in the two additional schools.

The classrooms for the two experimental groups were modified according to the ideas of Strauss and Lehtinen, in order to provide as far as possible a stimulus-free classroom environment. The classrooms for the control groups were not subject to any environmental alterations.

The four teachers and the teacher-assistants for the project were chosen with great care and before beginning the research period proper, all the teachers and teacher-assistants received special instructions in the specialized teaching methods designed for this study.

A very detailed account of these children, including their history, family background and results of the initial medical, neurological and psychiatric examinations, together with psychological test results and level of educational attainments, is given in the monograph. There is also a description of the environmental changes in the classroom arrangements, together with some details of teaching methods used with the experimental group.

The research team had drawn freely on what could be learnt from the work of Strauss and Lehtinen in the Cove Schools. Cruickshank himself had been for many years concerned with studying perception in cerebral palsy and findings from his various research studies (1957, 1951a, 1951b, 1951c, 1952) also influenced the approach to teaching the experimental groups.

Fundamental to the approach to teaching the experimental group was—(1) a stimulus-free environment, which involved the reduction of environmental space and the reduction of unessential visual and auditory environmental stimuli, (2) a careful structuring of the daily programme of activities, so that each child knew what was expected of him and what he could expect would be likely to happen to him, (3) increase of the stimulus value of the instructional materials themselves, (4) arranging for the teacher to know each child, what were his handicaps and his strengths, his limitations and his potentialities.

In the light of this awareness, a programme of instruction was planned for each child individually, with the special purpose of helping him to overcome the specific disabilities which would seem to underlie the difficulties in school learning. This included tasks designed to develop finer muscular control, eye–hand co-ordination, form perception and perception of figure–ground relationships.

It was thought important, therefore, that the child should be allowed to begin with work in which he was able to succeed, but that he should be led, by carefully thought-out developmental stages, through tasks that he found difficult, making sure that he had mastered each step before going on to the next. All approaches to learning—auditory, visual, kinaesthetic and tactile—were used in the highly structured programme of the experimental classes.

This teaching project lasted for one school year and thorough testing was carried out at the end of the 10 months' schooling. The experimental groups were combined for this re-testing and significant gains were noted in the ability of these children to withstand distractions, in the rate of development of social skills as measured by the Vineland Scale of Social Maturity and in fewer errors in such perceptual tests as the Bender Visual Gestalt test.

Follow-up testing was carried out 12 months later, after the children had spent the next year in ordinary classes. At the end of this second year, children who had been in the experimental classes did not score significantly better than the controls on any scoring category. The area of greatest improvement for all the children during the 2-year period was in academic achievement. There were no demonstrable differences between the combined experimental and control groups, though almost all the children had made substantial gains over the 2-year period.

The results of this research study are inconclusive. It may be that one year was too short a time for any permanent impact to be made on the adjustment and learning of such handicapped children. It is also probable that there were too many uncontrolled, or indeed uncontrollable variables in this study. Nevertheless, it is interesting that both the experimental and control groups made striking progress in educational achievement over the 2-year period. This suggests that the important influence for these children was that they were taught in very small classes, ten only in each, by teachers selected for their quality and experience and, equally important, for their intelligent understanding of the causes of these children's behavioural and learning difficulties.

On the basis of theories regarding special learning difficulties thought to be due to organic neurological impairment, a number of experimental schools have been started in the United States. It is not possible here to evaluate these in detail, but examples of these schools may be of interest.

A Pilot School for the Brain Injured Child was set up under the auspices of the University of Washington, Seattle. The approach in this school is described by Strother (1963), Professor of Psychology at the University and Director of the School. Strother, like others, deplores the looseness of the term "brain-injured" and that at present, the term is used, misleadingly, to designate children who exhibit certain patterns of behaviour and who present certain special learning problems. He suggests that the term "Strauss syndrome" would be more useful, since "syndrome" indicates that the children exhibit a characteristic combination of symptoms, while not necessarily implying that these symptoms are due to brain-injury. Strother holds that these children constitute a group which requires special techniques of psychological evaluation and special educational programming.

> From an educational point of view, the objective of an examination of the child is not to determine whether he is brain-injured, but to lay a foundation for the planning of an educational programme that will develop his abilities and compensate for his disabilities.

In making an educational diagnosis, Strother emphasizes the need for a systematic inventory of the child's levels of development in perception and motor functions, in communication, in concept formation and in social interaction and he stresses the value of a developmental profile. On the basis of this information, four fundamental principles are emphasized: (1) learning sequences should be broken down into small successive steps, (2) these steps should be so arranged and presented that the child responds successfully, (3) at any point at which the child has difficulty, the teacher should be prepared to intervene and to find some way of modifying this step to make it easier for the child, (4) these children will require more practice to learn a given step and more frequent review to retain it than is necessary for normal children.

Strother also believes, with Strauss and his followers, that too much space and environmental stimulation increases these children's hyperactivity and that they need not only structured physical space, but also structured learning programmes. It is this emphasis on structure, together with carefully programmed conditioning, that characterizes most American school projects for the so-called "brain-injured" child.

The Pathway School in Pennsylvania is mainly concerned with helping aphasic and brain-damaged children and furthering understanding of these two categories of children, whose learning difficulties are often severe. In 1964, under the editorship of Rappaport, the Director of the Pathway School, a symposium of the results of discussions regarding the characteristics of aphasia in children and of the brain damage syndrome was published and this was followed by a second volume (1965), in which an attempt was made to clarify differential diagnosis.

The approach to teaching the aphasic child at the Pathway School is based on McGinnis's (1963) Association Method. She has described this method very fully in her book on *Aphasic Children*. The Volta Bureau have also published pamphlets dealing with this subject and one written by McGinnis (1960) and colleagues at the Central Institute for the Deaf, St. Louis, explains very clearly the principles underlying this method of teaching aphasic children. The approach to teaching so-called brain-damaged children is greatly influenced by the work of Cruickshank, but Rappaport also stresses the need of the brain-damaged child for help in ego development and his approach to work with these children draws heavily on psychoanalytical ego psychology. He holds that this group of children not only need the help of a structured school programme, but also the support of psycho-therapy in most cases.

In her School of Educational Therapy in Los Angeles, Frostig lays great emphasis on testing as a basis for educational therapy. Particularly for the children with learning difficulties whom she seeks to help, she re-emphasizes the importance of a constant recognition of individual differences. In an interesting paper given to a Conference on the Assessment of the Cerebral Palsied Child for Education, Frostig (1968) shows the careful thought that has gone into her use of her own, together with certain other diag-nostic tests, in order to reveal the pattern of assets and liabilities unique for each individual child and on which the plan for teach-ing can be based. Frostig, as the good educationist she is, also stresses that choice of educational procedures made on the basis of this initial testing should not be regarded as final, but expects the sensitive observation of teachers to contribute and, where necessary, change or modify the course of teaching for each individual child. In this paper, she discusses and explains very thoughtfully her rationale for the use of the tests chosen as a basis for educational therapy.

Frostig bases much of her remedial teaching on her programme for the development of visual perception. She and her co-workers have developed a teaching programme for the development of visual perception in the five areas of visual perception, levels of which are assessed in the Frostig Developmental Test of Visual Perception, described above. These are the areas of visual percep-tual abilities which Frostig believes to have the greatest relevance to school learning. Though a major part of the work books are graded paper and pencil tasks, Frostig insists that sensori-motor training should precede and accompany perceptual training through work books. Because Frostig believes that the ability to perceive spatial relationships grows out of the earlier ability to perceive the position of an object in relation to one's own body, she includes many graded exercises to develop body image, body concept and body schema. She also regards it as important that the children should learn to differentiate right from left. Throughout the whole programme of work books, Frostig lays great stress on active and practical exercises as the basis for perceptual development.

This also is the basic thesis in the method expounded by Kephart (1960) in *The Slow Learner in The Classroom*. He has built up very carefully worked out series of exercises to develop a child's visuo-motor skills, stresses the importance of recognizing the need for "readiness" to begin learning and has developed ways of fostering it in the slow learner. Throughout his book, he stresses that:

> Teaching should be directed toward the total activity of the child in any given task. The total activity includes all four processes: input, integration, output and feed-back. If any of these processes are deficient, the child may be expected to experience difficulty. . . . The too frequent dichotomy between muscular or motor activities and intellectual activities becomes untenable. Since we cannot separate the perceptual and the motor in the processes of the child, we should not attempt to separate them in teaching him.

Others go further than this, for example Delacato (1963) writing of *Diagnosis and Treatment of Speech and Reading Problems*, from the Developmental Reading Programme Rehabilitation Centre, Philadelphia, claims that "by improving the child's neurological organisation we make his receptive abilities more efficient", and again he holds that the speech and reading problems of children arise from their "inadequate neurological organisation because they were pushed by their parents, for example, to walk before they were neurologically ready to walk". At the time of writing, I am not aware of any controlled research studies that evaluate the claims made for the methods described by Delacato and his co-workers.

More recently, Cruickshank (1966) and some eighteen specialists in various disciplines met to discuss the kind of training it is necessary for teachers to have if they are to approach this work with neurologically handicapped children adequately. These discussions are published under Cruickshank's editorship.

The situation in Britain, which has a more cohesive society, is somewhat different. It is the legal responsibility of local education authorities to provide education for all the educable children living in their area and this includes all categories of handicapped children.

Ten categories are listed in the *Handicapped Pupils and Special Schools Regulations, 1959*". These are children who, because of the nature of their handicaps, require special educational treatment. They are defined as follows:

(a) blind pupils, that is to say, pupils who have no sight or whose sight is or is likely to become so defective that they require education by methods not involving the use of sight;

(b) partially sighted pupils, that is to say, pupils who by reason of defective vision cannot follow the normal regime of ordinary schools without detriment to their sight or to their educational development, but can be educated by special methods involving the use of sight;

(c) deaf pupils, that is to say, pupils with impaired hearing who require education by methods suitable for pupils with little or no naturally acquired speech or language;

(d) partially deaf pupils, that is to say, pupils with impaired hearing whose development of speech and language, even if retarded, is following a normal pattern and who require for their education special arrangements or facilities though not necessarily all the educational methods used for deaf pupils;

(e) educationally subnormal pupils, that is to say, pupils who by reason of limited ability or other conditions resulting in educational retardation, require some specialised form of education wholly or partly in substitution for the education normally given in ordinary schools;

(f) epileptic pupils, that is to say, pupils who by reason of epilepsy cannot be educated under the normal regime of ordinary schools without detriment to themselves or other pupils;

(g) maladjusted pupils, that is to say, pupils who show evidence of emotional instability or psychological disturbance and require special educational treatment in order to effect their personal, social or educational readjustment;

(h) physically handicapped pupils, that is to say, pupils not suffering solely from a defect of sight or hearing who by reason of disease or crippling defect cannot, without detriment to their health or educational development be satisfactorily educated under the normal regime of ordinary schools;

(i) pupils suffering from speech defect, that is to say, pupils who on

account of defect or lack of speech not due to deafness require special
educational treatment; and
(j) delicate pupils, that is to say, pupils not falling under any other category in this regulation, who by reason of impaired physical condition
need a change of environment or cannot, without risk to their health
or educational development, be educated under the normal regime of
ordinary schools.

There is as yet no special category of children whose difficulties
in school learning are thought to be due to organic neurological
impairment, though there is a growing awareness of the fact that
these children exist and are possibly not being adequately catered
for. It is largely from work with cerebral palsied children that an
awareness of the needs of some children with very slight physical
handicap but severe specific learning difficulties has arisen. Most
education authorities make some provision for children who,
though normally intelligent, are falling behind in school work.
They are usually catered for in small classes or units, which
children from a group of schools in an area can attend. A good
deal of work of an experimental nature is now being done in local
authority special schools and classes, using some of the Kephart,
Strauss, Frostig and other similar remedial techniques, though I
know of none in Britain where the methods are applied with the
strict rigidity that would appear to characterize some of the
programming of learning tasks used in many American schools
for "remediation" of brain-injured children.

More recently, the Inner London Education Authority
appointed a peripatetic teacher of neurologically handicapped
children. She had had training as an "educational therapist" at
the Frostig School in Los Angeles and started by working in three
London schools—one a school for physically handicapped
children, one for educationally subnormal and one for maladjusted
children. She used the Frostig methods in tutoring children,
either individually or in small groups and discussed their problems with class teachers. This was a tentative approach, in order
to find out whether the problems of these neurologically handicapped children were being overlooked. She has now trained three
other teachers in the use of the Frostig method and while

experiments show some progress in the children having this extra help, it is important to note that teachers taking part are all "special" teachers, who do not have a narrow conception of the place of perceptual training so that the experiment does not rigidly control other factors that may have helped those children.

A more carefully designed research experiment to assess the value of remedial visuo-motor training arose directly out of a multi-disciplinary research on vision and perception, carried out at a school for physically handicapped children under a research team led by Abercrombie (1964). This was made possible by a grant from the Spastic's Society. One of the psychologists, Dr. Tyson, who helped in this research and who is particularly interested in this kind of remedial education, undertook some experimental remedial training in the research study of a small number of the children who showed pronounced visual–perceptual and visuo-motor difficulties. Tyson based her remedial programme on the Frostig remedial work-books for visual perception training. Although this pilot study of the value of remedial visuo-motor training involved only a small number of children, it was designed and carried out with great care and vision. Tyson is herself obviously a gifted and enthusiastic teacher and her description (1963) of the study, of her methods and of the materials she used, merits careful reading for any who are concerned to find ways of helping children whose learning problems appear to be related to difficulties in visuo-spatial perception.

This pilot study of remedial visuo-motor training extended over nearly a whole school year. The training was based on the use of Frostig's work-books for training in—(1) Eye-motor Co-ordination, (2) Figure–Ground Perception, (3) Constancy of Perception of Space and Size, (4) Position in Space and (5) Perception of Spatial Relationships.

Frostig herself stresses that none of the work-books should be attempted until the child has had ample practice through physical exercises with three-dimensional objects. Examples of Tyson's own preliminary "play exercises", before introduction to pencil and paper work in eye-motor co-ordination, are shown below.

The pencil and paper tasks require the child to follow paths of increasing complexity and gradually decreasing width (examples shown in Fig. 15, page 111). The four illustrations in Fig. 34 show the kind of play material exercises designed to give the child preliminary practice in eye-motor co-ordination. In these exercises, the child was required to "drive" the car on the "road"

Fig. 34a

Fig. 34b

drawn on a blackboard placed horizontally on a low table. In the first task (Fig. 34a) the child was required to "drive" the car on a wide straight "road". When he could manage this without allowing the car to touch the verge, the roads were gradually made narrower and more bends and curves were introduced. Similar exercises involving keeping trains *on* railway lines were given.

Fig. 34c.

Fig. 34d.

Then, two intersecting roads were drawn, of two different colours, for example red and green. The child was required to "drive" a red car down the red "road" and a green car down the green "road" (Fig. 34b). As the child became competent in this kind of task, the help given by using different colours was dispensed with (Fig. 34d).

FIG. 35.

Exercises in preparation for the figure–ground work-book started with practice in very simple discriminations on the game "Find the Stranger", such as a red brick in a group of green bricks, or a larger red bead in a group of smaller ones, or a round bead in a group of square ones (Plate 3). These are simple examples of the very carefully graded play material used by Tyson in her study of the value of remedial training techniques. Tyson also used various techniques to help the children to develop a sense of direction and orientation. Practice in assembling a manikin (Fig. 35) was followed by the use of a jointed figure (Fig. 36) on which body parts could be identified and movements could be demonstrated and then copied by the child.

Much of Tyson's "play" material is similar to what would be found in any good infant school, but it had the importance here of being based on ordered and carefully worked-out remedial principles and used on a very individual basis.

Fig. 36.

In order to evaluate the effect of the remedial training, the children were tested at the beginning and end of the period on tests which are thought to involve certain aspects of visuo-motor performance. Tests used were block design and object assembly sub-tests of the W.I.S.C., Frostig's Developmental Test of Visual Perception, Zazzo's adaptations of the Bender Gestalt and Kohs Blocks test, Goldstein Scheerer Sticks test and the Neale Test of Reading Ability.

Although Tyson is very cautious in the conclusions she draws from work with so small a number of children, she found in the "experimental" children's improvement on their earlier scores, as compared with that of the control children, that the trends shown were promising. The difference in the test scores was significant at the 5 per cent level. This group of children ranged in age from 8 years 5 months to 13 years 6 months. The most striking improvement was seen in the youngest boy of the group (8 years 5 months). It is probable that the value of this kind of training would be increased if used with younger children.

Tyson is currently experimenting in ways of helping young children who have primarily language retardation, but who also seem to be generally immature all round and appear to need help also in developing perceptual, visuo-motor and motor abilities.

She tried first with a "Head start" class for five weeks during the summer holidays, in which teachers, volunteer student helpers and speech therapists combined to help a few of these children. The success of this project has led her to provide a similar class on a more regular basis. Although there has not yet been time to reach any conclusive results, many professional people who are concerned in other ways with the children have been impressed by the improvements they have observed.

Voluntary societies in Britain have set up and maintain some special schools, which are used on a fee-paying arrangement by local education authorities. A number of schools for cerebral palsied children grew up in this way through the Spastics' Society. Considerable work with experimental teaching methods for so-called "clumsy" children have centred round the Percy Hedley Cerebral Palsy School in Newcastle and at that same school, a study of the value of Frostig's training methods is being carried out by Harker (1966). His results at present are tentative, but appear promising.

A project designed—(1) to detect the incidence of children with minimal cerebral dysfunction in the normal junior school population and (2) to plan suitable remedial methods—has been carried out by Dr. A. Bowley (1969),* Psychologist at Cheyne Walk

* I am indebted to Dr. Bowley for lending me a copy of her paper and allowing me to quote from it prior to its publication.

School for Cerebral Palsied Children in London and at the Children's Unit, Belmont Hospital, Surrey.

She started first with a pilot study in three junior schools in the Borough of Kensington and Chelsea, which were selected as being representative of a cross-section of the junior schools population in the borough. After making a personal contact with the schools to explain the purpose of the project, the Heads, in collaboration with their staffs, were asked to complete a simple questionnaire on each child, concerning such everyday skills as the use of tools, drawing, writing, speech and reading and physical education. The total number of pupils in the three schools selected was 646. On the basis of information gained from these questionnaires, those children who showed five or more of the nine characteristics listed were offered appointments for psychological assessment at the Cheyne Centre.

The psychological assessment was based on the following battery of tests:

1. W.I.S.C. Performance Scale I.Q.
2. W.I.S.C. Vocabulary Test—expressive vocabulary.
3. English Picture Vocabulary—verbal comprehension.
4. Illinois test of Psycho-linguistic abilities.
5. Reading Age (Burt or Holborn Scale).
6. Arithmetic Age (W.I.S.C. Oral Test).
7. Frostig Perception Test.
8. Bender Gestalt Designs.
9. Benton Visual Retention Test.
10. Hand and Eye Dominance.

A brief history of the child's development, his milestones and illnesses was obtained from the mother. School attendance was noted as good or bad. Any medical attention, such as prescription of glasses or hearing aid or any operation was noted. When clumsiness, restlessness or difficulty in manual skills was very marked, neurological vetting was arranged. Ten children from the three schools were selected on the basis of this diagnostic assessment. From a junior school population of 646, this means an incidence of $1\frac{1}{2}$ per cent. Following this pilot study, the survey was extended to all those junior schools in the borough who were willing to co-operate. The final study is based on a school population of 2280 children, of whom thirty-four, that is 1·49 per cent, had disabilities in reading and writing, language development or manual dexterity which retarded educational progress, though they were of normal intelligence.

The children who were included in the study had an I.Q. range of 80–113. With children of lower intelligence, it was felt that poor intelligence in such cases was the major factor in educational retardation, although visuo-spatial difficulties most probably also played a part. Language retardation was noted in all the children. She found also marked weakness in visual and auditory memory, as tested in the Auditory–Vocal Sequencing and Visuo-motor Sequencing in the Illinois Test of Psycho-linguistic abilities. All the children were retarded in reading by 1 or 2 years, two of them being 4 years retarded.

Bowley summarized the probable causal factors of severe reading disability in five of the cases studied:

1. Language retardation (four cases).
2. Weakness in auditory and visual memory (auditory-vocal sequencing and visuo-motor sequencing) (four cases).
3. Left-hand/eye dominance (two cases).
4. Minor visuo-spatial difficulties (two cases).
5. Periods of non-attendance in infant school (two cases).
6. Minimal neurological dysfunction (two cases).
7. Slight physical immaturity and minor congenital deformities (one case).

On the evidence of the psychological assessment, together with that of the neurological examination, Bowley drew the conclusion that although delayed language development, late talking, limited vocabulary, poor auditory or visual memory and sequencing were the most evident single causes of reading retardation in this group, there were other factors suggestive of minimal cerebral dysfunction affecting speech development, motor control, manual dexterity and perception, which clearly handicapped the child in speed and accuracy of learning.

From her experience in giving remedial teaching help for these children, Bowley suggested that a "three-pronged" attack on the children's problems attained the best results: that is, (1) careful programmed teaching, designed to meet the special needs of the individual child, (2) supplementary to (1), speech therapy directed to improving vocabulary and language skills and (3) occupational therapy to improve motor co-ordination, manual dexterity and perception.

During the period in which this remedial programme has been in operation, that is three school terms, Bowley has noticed "quite a dramatic improvement in reading and in the children's general attitude". This is confirmed by her follow-up test results. She stresses the need for *special* remedial steps to be taken at an early age and says: "It is my contention that ordinary global teaching using a combination of methods, phonic or visual, in a class group, however skilled the teacher, cannot achieve quick results with these children".

I have described this study in some detail because it represents so well the contribution that can be made to this very difficult subject by the initiative and work of one psychologist, in collaboration with medical specialists and teachers, on a very individual basis. Other psychologists may feel that they would approach this problem in a different way, using a different battery of tests or different remedial teaching methods, but there is room for much more research before many of the questions raised by this controversial subject of the methods of identification and teaching of neurologically impaired children can be clarified.

Although the main concern of this book is with identification and methods of helping children of normal intelligence who are found to have specific learning disabilities, it is sometimes the case that similar difficulties are found in children who are educationally subnormal.

While modifying the pace of learning to the needs of a globally slow learning child, it should also be recognized that the mentally subnormal child who has also specific difficulties arising from disordered perceptual development can be helped by careful training in perceptual tasks. During his work at the Manor Hospital, Epsom, Clarke demonstrated in a vivid and practical way the extent to which imbeciles who had been institutionalized for many years could be taught. Writing of this, he says (1961)—"We now have strong experimental evidence that the common perceptual deficiencies can be ameliorated by relatively short periods of individual training". And he continues, "The imbecile's response to proper perceptual training is often remarkable, and some 9-year-old imbecile children have been brought up to the perceptual ability in complex discrimination tasks of trained adults of the same mental grade".

While it is important not to overlook the need of special help in areas of deviant development in severely backward children, it is equally important not to be misled by very severe specific learning disability in a normally intelligent child, so that we fail to recognize his urgent need of special help in a specific area of development and relegate him to a special school for children who are educationally subnormal in a global way, where his total educational needs cannot be met.

There is in this country a gradual, but quite definite move to make provision for speech handicapped children and children with language and communication problems. Until fairly recently, educational provision for children with specific language defects was available only at the Moor House Residential School for children from 5 to 16 years of age. This school, the first of its kind in the country, has a team of specialists for the complete investigation of speech defective children. The team consists of neurologist, psychiatrist, otologist, plastic surgeon, educational psychologist and speech therapists. Consultations with a neuro-surgeon and a paediatrician are also available. Children are usually admitted to the in-patient diagnostic section of the school for about a week before a decision regarding treatment and educational provision is made. There is now also the John Horniman Residential School for Children Suffering from Speech Defects. This caters for children aged 5–9 years and is maintained by the Invalid Children's Aid Association.

In 1962, the I.C.A.A. also opened the Edith Edwards House School for maladjusted children with communication difficulties. The children in this school are estimated to be of average intelligence or above and their speech difficulties are not, in so far as can be ascertained, due to any organic disability. These children show a great variety of behaviour problems, ranging from deep withdrawal in some to almost uncontrollable aggressive and destructive behaviour in others. Many of them show the obsessional ritualistic behaviour characteristic of autistic children. Their lack of communication is thought to be a symptom and not the cause of their emotional problems. For this reason, they are not thought to be suitably helped in schools for children with speech defects. Their speech and learning problems are very different from those of children with organic damage.

Local education authorities more actively aware of the importance of normal development of speech and communication in young children are setting up units where children needing it can be helped early.

In September 1963, Bristol Education Committee set up a Delayed Speech Unit. This unit is in an ordinary nursery school, but has one teacher and two nursery assistants to a maximum of ten children. The approach is similar to that of a normal nursery school, except that the teacher takes individual children for "language" sessions and an individual child can, if necessary, have almost continuous contact with an adult. It is basic that children initially learn the use of language from adults. Observational study of non-talking and isolated children in a normal nursery school confirmed that until young children have developed the beginnings of language in relation with an adult, they are not able to learn it, nor indeed take part in social play with the children in the nursery group. It is the policy in this speech defective unit to return the child to a normal group as soon as he is sufficiently mature and fluent to mix and benefit from it. It is usually around this time that speech therapy can suitably begin.

Specific language disability is defined by Morley (1965) as: "delayed or absent language development (involving expression and/or comprehension), in the absence of marked hearing loss or mental or psychogenic retardation".

The incidence of this defect has been the subject of several sample surveys. In her Newcastle Sample of 114 children, Morley found that at 3 years 9 months, 1 per cent of the children had "limited or poor use of language". In investigation of incidence based on referral rates, Ingram (1964) concludes that prevalence of speech defect in children between 3 and 10 years might be one per 1000 children. In 1964 a sample survey of one in ten Bristol children in the age-range 2 years 4 months to 4 years 3 months, produced three children whose language defect was sufficiently specific and severe to require their being placed in the delayed speech unit. This suggested that in this age-range, there might be thirty children with these needs in Bristol, giving a prevalence estimate of $4 \cdot 1$ per 1000. Wedell (1966) suggested that for a variety of sampling reasons this should be regarded as a minimal estimate for that age-range. Other similar surveys have been carried out in Croydon, Nottingham, Aberdeen and Glasgow. Classes in various local authority areas are being set up to provide suitable education for these children. Apart from the two residential schools, Moor House and the John Horniman School, it seems probable that up to some 3 or 4 years ago, the majority of children with specific language defects were placed in classes or schools for educationally subnormal children or schools for the deaf. In the last 4 years, a number of day classes have been set up. These are generally established in ordinary primary schools, so that the children are not completely segregated from speaking children, with whom they can mix for other activities and in play. The classes usually have up to ten children, from nursery school age upwards, in the charge of a qualified teacher with one or more assistants. Class activity has to be geared to the needs of each child and individual help in language development forms an important part of each day's programme.

Many of the methods used with these children are based on

methods of teaching aphasic children used and demonstrated in the United States, such, for example, as Barry's (1961) *Evaluation and Training of the Young Aphasic Child*, and McGinnis's (1963) *Identification and Education of Aphasic Children by the Association Method*. Most of these classes have not been running for sufficiently long to provide significant assessment of their results, but it is expected that many of the children, helped early in this way, will later be able to take their place in ordinary schools.

In the United States, similar units are frequently organized under the sponsorship and guidance of University Departments. In the University of Wisconsin, for example, the department concerned with language and communication disorders has its own pre-school clinic for children with language disorders. Children with very severe disorders of communication find here a friendly and stimulating atmosphere. Although language experience and practice for these children is carefully planned, for the children it was a free and happy place which when I visited it, appeared to me to offer ample opportunity for the child to develop language and grow in experience of its use, without undue pressure. Most of the children attending this clinic–nursery school are 5 or 6 years of age. In that community at any rate, they are rarely identified before the age when they would normally start to attend kindergarten at 5 years or formal schooling at 6.

In the North Western University, Evanston, Chicago, Myklebust and his colleague Miss Johnson (1967) head a very large centre for treatment of children with language disorders. Here, Myklebust seeks to make a clear distinction between those children whose language disorder arises from loss of hearing and those whom he believes to have a central nervous system disorder of an aphasic nature.

Myklebust is investigating the use of electronic devices which test and record children's visual and auditory discrimination and produce an E.E.G. record while the child is actively carrying out perceptual tasks. Myklebust and his co-workers expect through such recordings to produce evidence of previously undetected minimal brain injury. Myklebust also initiated a screening procedure, carried out in local schools. This is designed to ascertain those children who are under-achieving and, where the parents are willing to co-operate, the children are then taken into a research study. Suitable teaching methods are carefully investigated and the major principles involved in this are described in some detail in the book by Johnson and Myklebust (1967) on educational principles and practices relevant to learning disabilities.

Dyslexia

The situation regarding developmental dyslexia is not so clear. On a grant from the Invalid Children's Aid Association, a centre in London has been established for a 5-year research project into the study and treatment of specific developmental dyslexia. This "Word-Blind Centre" is concerned mainly with identification and diagnosis and remedial teaching of these so-called word-blind children. The situation in Britain is still confused and the subject of much controversy. It is of value, therefore, that the I.C.A.A. has, by means of a grant to the National Bureau of Co-operation in Child Care, made it possible for a careful survey of their large sample of carefully documented cases to be analysed, in order to get clearer evidence of the incidence of this condition in this country.

The results of this survey, presented as an analysis of *Seven-year-olds who cannot Read*, are being prepared for publication in the National Bureau's series, "Studies in Child Development" by Kellmer Pringle and others.

In 1960 a survey was undertaken under the auspices of the Chief Medical Officer of the Department of Education and Science in order to determine whether, among the children who are severely delayed in reading, a specific condition does exist and if so, how frequently it occurs. This investigation was carried out by a school medical officer and a preliminary report based on the examination of 225 children is published in detail (1961) in the Chief Medical Officer's *Health of the School Child, 1960 and 1961*. In the 1965–6 report on the *Health of the School Child*, the final report on completion of the survey is presented. This stresses the complicated underlying causes of reading delay in children, despite their normal intelligence. Since more careful medical supervision of school children has reduced the frequency of undetected visual and hearing defects, the final findings of the survey suggests that much commoner factors in reading delay are strephosymbolia (defined here as confusion of laterality due to delayed neuro-physiological maturation), poor auditory memory and primary emotional disturbance. In view of the importance of this subject, the Department of Education and Science gave a research grant in 1965 to Professor Meredith of the Department of Psychology of Leeds University to investigate the subject further. His final report on this study is not yet produced.

Perhaps the most comprehensive studies of dyslexia have been made in the Scandinavian countries. In a recent study of 74 children in the Word-blind Institute in Copenhagen, it was thought that dyslexia was genetically determined in 63 per cent of the cases. A further 7 per cent of the cases had a history of encephalitis, in 13 per cent there was a history of some difficulty in the neo-natal period and 10 per cent gave a history of complication during pregnancy. In the study of children attending the Word-blind Institute in Copenhagen, there is increasing evidence that dyslexia is a disorder due to deviant maturation and is more often genetically determined than the result of minimal brain damage. Hansen (1966) also emphasizes the increasing evidence for the relationship between developmental dyslexia and speech and language disorders.

With very few exceptions, the experiments in teaching and the research projects into identification and incidence of children with special learning disorders outlined in this chapter have been concerned with children who have already started school and encountered troubles and difficulties. Clearly, it is a matter of urgency that these children should be identified early, so that they can be helped before they experience difficulty at school, with all the concomitant emotional distress that accompanies failure and inability to keep up with their peers in school work.

CHAPTER 7

The Outlook for the Future

THE skilled help of many disciplines is required in the treatment of children with specific learning disabilities. In this book, however, my concern has been primarily with the particular contribution of the psychologist to the service of these children.

What should this contribution be? It falls mainly, I suggest, under the following headings:

1. Diagnostic assessment.
2. Consideration of the school placement in the light of this diagnostic assessment, in order to judge the value and suitability of the school opportunities that the child is getting.
3. Collaboration with the child's teachers in working out a suitable programme, through which the assets he possesses can be used to offset, or if this is possible, circumvent his disabilities.
4. Continuing re-assessment and through this, in co-operation with the teachers, consideration of the value of the teaching methods being used and where necessary a change in method.
5. Scientific assessments of the value of psychological tests in the diagnostic work and of teaching programmes and teaching methods based on diagnostic findings. These judgements can only be validated through research that is carefully designed and carried out by experimental psychologists. The psychologist working in the field needs to have close contacts with the work of experimental

psychologists, so that their findings can be brought to the teacher and specialized knowledge of the two disciplines interrelated, so as to feed each other.

Assessment

From the study of the patterns of learning disorder demonstrated in this book, it can be seen that in many of the children showing such patterns, there is no neurological impairment such as can be demonstrated by positive neurological signs. Nor, in many of these children, is there anything in the birth history or aetiology to suggest that the learning difficulties may be due to brain injury. It is the case, however, that many children whose special learning disorders or excessively distractible behaviour have caused them to be brought to the notice of a psychologist for advice and help, show the same kinds of patterns in learning and behaviour, of assets and disabilities, on psychological testing, as do those children who are known to have a history of neurological impairment. In the research study reported here of the 3- and 4-year-old children in whom cerebral dysfunction and an estimate of its severity was recorded at birth, the ratings of behavioural characteristics, particularly in the 3-year-olds, distinguished the cases from the controls more significantly than did the tests. As would be expected, the very severely damaged showed damage globally and they have remained to date subnormal, damaged children. But among those children whose damage was less severe, some now in their second year in school cannot be distinguished from normally developing children, while others, the severity of whose damage was matched with them by the paediatrician who knew these children and made the record of them at birth, were showing definite and characteristic learning problems despite the fact that they were normally intelligent children.

There is no doubt that among children who are known to have suffered cerebral damage at or around birth, certain patterns of learning disorder exist and/or some characteristic behaviours and also often mild motor inco-ordination. It is now generally agreed that such a condition exists among some children without recognizable cerebral palsy, even though it is not possible to relate it to known neurological impairment.

It is not, however, the function of the psychologist to decide that a child is "brain-injured" on the evidence of psychological tests alone. Pointers to this condition may be thought to be so strong in the psychological tests used that the need for a neurological investigation is considered desirable. But whether the child is found medically to be neuro-developmentally impaired or not, the psychological assessment of the child serves a separate and different purpose.

It has increasingly been realized that there are many deviant rates and patterns of functioning among the many types of handicapped children. The need to cater adequately for these variously handicapped children has, in its turn, influenced the kind of approach made by the psychologist to the use of tests as part of the diagnostic assessment procedure. Psychologists working in hospital among children with severe language disorders, autistic children, severely handicapped hydrocephalics, cerebral palsied children and others, quickly feel dissatisfaction with the idea of trying to make a useful contribution to management or education, in terms of a global I.Q. which for most of such children carries little meaning. Assessments for these handicapped children are not required in order to compare their level of total functioning with that of their normal fellows. A psychological assessment for such children seeks to draw up a blueprint, as it were, of the patterning of the child's mental functioning. We are not comparing one child with another, but comparing the levels of functioning within the child himself, in order to have a guide to his own disabilities and strengths, and to weigh up these factors against his physical condition in all areas of functioning, so that we can try to judge in what ways a weakness can be supported or modified by his strengths.

With some very badly handicapped children, or with children whose rates of maturation show marked deviations in certain areas, this is not easy. It often takes a long time. With young pre-school handicapped children, a really useful assessment can only be made over a period involving careful observation of the infant in a nursery group or school. While weaning ourselves away from complete satisfaction with the use of a well-standardized intelligence test, whose strengths and weaknesses we have come to know well, it is important in our exploration into the use of other kinds of tests and measures that we do not lose sight of the need to retain scientific accuracy and integrity. In the need to find accurate and useful new techniques of testing and investigation, in order to pattern the deviant child's levels of mental functioning, it is necessary that we should understand a great deal more than we do at present about the meaning of the kinds of ability that we believe the test to assess.

This, then, is one exciting challenge to psychologists: through rigorous experimentation and carefully designed research projects, to refine and improve diagnostic procedure so as to be able to give better and more reliable advice on management and education.

Management and Education of Children with Neuro-developmental Learning Disorders

For more than 20 years Britain has had the benefit of legislation providing for special educational treatment for children whose handicap places them in one of the categories listed in Chapter 6. The best method of dealing with problems of educating children with specific learning disorders would not, however, seem to lie in creating yet another category, in which they could be set apart for "special educational provision". The past 10 years have taught us much about these children and although we need to learn a great deal more, it is already plain that the most important thing to remember is the need to recognize the individual differences in these children. If psychological assessment is to make a really valuable contribution to helping in their training and education, it must begin from each individual child. Most of these children cannot be catered for in groups. Individual teaching by skilled teachers who understand and recognize each child's individual areas of inadequacy is a first essential, if he is to be helped to the stage where he can take part in group learning.

Methods of learning, like indeed the whole field of learning theory as applicable to these children, are full of as yet unanswered problems. This century has seen considerable research into the ways in which children learn. In the United States education is still, in a great measure, dominated by a behaviourist view of learning theory and strongly influenced by such theorists as Skinner. Programmed learning with operant conditioning and a great deal of stress on the place of reinforcement and the importance of consistent rewards are held to be highly relevant to the ways by which children learn. To such a degree is this the case, in fact, that in some schools where this type of approach to learning was rigidly maintained, it has seemed to the present writer that the place and contribution of the teacher was almost entirely lost sight of.

More dominant in Great Britain is a learning theory which reflects the influence in work with young children of great teachers like Susan Isaacs, subsequently reinforced by the ideas of Piaget. This is based on the recognition that learning takes place through a continuous process of interaction between the learner and his environment, and is well summarized in the Plowden Report (1968) as follows:

> Activity and experience, both physical and mental, are often the best means of gaining knowledge and acquiring facts . . . facts are best retained when they are used and understood . . . when understanding has been achieved, consolidation should follow. At this stage children profit from various types of practice devised by their teachers and from direct instruction.

This philosophy places the teacher firmly in the centre of the stage. To quote again from the Plowden Report: "By their practical work in the classroom, teachers have perhaps as much to contribute to psychology as the psychologists to educational practice."

The present writer shares the Plowden Committee's belief. Yet there is clearly need for very much more research into the learning processes through which damaged children can be helped to learn and most teachers welcome help and advice on the value of their methods and approach. The problem is that educational psychologists are generally too involved in day-to-day commitments of work to have time for the actual setting up and carrying out of research projects, and the experimental psychologist to whom such research can reasonably fall is often quite divorced from the child at school and his teacher. It is important that the relation between research and practice should be a two-way process. Particularly is this so in the sort of study required to carry out successful teaching projects with such deviant developers as the children discussed here. For success in this field, research and practice must be parts of a whole, each depending on the other.

It is difficult to find in adequate numbers teachers equipped to give the individual help many of these children urgently need, but much could perhaps be learned from the experience of the enthusiastic teachers who work in schools for cerebral-palsied children. The Spastic's Society regularly organizes study groups on education, assessment and other problems arising from work with cerebral-palsied children. To these conferences are invited not only the teachers, psychologists, doctors and therapists working in the Society's own schools, but interested research workers, who give and gain much in interchange of information and experience. Such study conferences ensure that what has been learned as a result both of research and through day-to-day experience is available to the representatives of many disciplines. The mutual exchange is stimulating and enriching. This procedure could usefully be copied.

There is general agreement as to the value of large-scale studies of the problems that arise in a school population. But the importance of such comprehensive studies as the Isle of Wight Survey, carried out under the London Institute of Education in the Department of Child Development, of the vast amount of information collected and analysed by the National Bureau for Co-operation in Child Care, or of the many useful research projects carried out under the auspices of the National Foundation for Educational Research, should not cause us to lose sight of the permanent need for valuable information that can only be obtained through carefully planned intimate studies of smaller numbers of children, and even, on occasion, of the functioning of individual children.

The research study reported on here has raised many questions to which it is important to find an answer, if adequate help is to be given to pre-school children who are showing signs of what appear to be neurodevelopmental disorders. Among these are:

> How and just when does the transition from naming to the use of true symbolic language occur?
>
> Is it possible to help a child to develop symbolic thought?
>
> What methods can be used to foster this in a child who is lagging in symbolic thinking?
>
> How early does a child begin to develop sequential skills?
>
> How can a child be helped in this development?
>
> Can a young child be helped to integrate his use of language with the carrying out of other tasks requiring different skills? Is there a "best age" for this and how can this integration best be accomplished?
>
> Can we help a child by "programming" to overcome maturational lags, or does external interference prove more damaging than leaving the child to develop at his own pace?
>
> Similarly, to what extent can a "clumsy" inco-ordinated child be helped by physio-therapy and exercises to overcome his motor defect? Or, alternatively, is it more advantageous to the child to be given extensive opportunities through free play and movement to develop through normal growth experiences?

If we knew more about these things, we might be better able to help the pre-school child before he is called upon to face the ordinary stresses of formal school.

Many other problems which still need resolving will occur to psychologists and teachers who work with young children. There are many gaps in our knowledge which need to be filled and which are perhaps most likely to be filled by intimate research studies, scientifically planned and carried out. When the recommendations of the Plowden Report are effectively implemented, there will be much more nursery school provision for young children. This could, and I hope will, provide an opportunity for psychologists to *observe* the young child and, together with his teachers, enter a whole new and exciting field of exploration. If profitably used, the opportunities thus provided can greatly enrich our understanding of child development and increase our ability to help in both preventive and constructive ways. Let us hope they will be taken.

CHAPTER 8

Results from a Follow-up of Children studied at 3 to 4 years of age (described in Chapter 3)

THIS follow-up study was designed to assess the value of the findings arising from the earlier research study in which the results of tests and rating scales were thought to be possible pointers to the identification of pre-school children who were likely to have learning disabilities when faced with formal schooling.

The children were seen in the original study at 3 to 4 years of age. The study then consisted of 44 "Cases"—that is children who were diagnosed at birth as having suffered some neurological damage in varying degrees of severity. These were compared in the study with 63 "Controls" who had also been born in the same hospitals and had a normal birth history and no severe or damaging illness up to their fourth year of life.

Plan for Follow-up

The children who were chosen as "Cases" in the original study had been noted at birth as showing some neurological distress which was thought likely to lead to some neurological dysfunction with the possible concomitant of learning difficulties during formal school life. The plan for follow-up, therefore, was designed to assess general overall intellectual functioning, to measure attainment in the basic subjects of reading and number and a test of the ability to perceive relationships relatively independent of verbal ability and of educational attainments.

Because the level of a child's attainment in basic school subjects is inevitably influenced not only by the child's inherent ability, but also by the quality of teaching and his school and home environment during his early school years, an attempt was

175

made to formulate an assessment of pertinent factors. We realized that this would be extremely difficult to carry out with any great reliability, so that it was decided that in preference to giving the teacher a form to fill up, the actual information should be obtained by the research assistant on her visit to the school. The schools of the children living in the London area were all visited by the research assistant, herself a trained Educational Psychologist. The schools of the children living in the Guildford area were visited by an Educational Psychologist working in the Surrey area. Two children who had moved to Cornwall were assessed and the schools and homes visited by the Educational Psychologist working in that area, as was also a child living in Wiltshire.*

Form used for School Visits

1. ATTENDANCE

Good . . . frequent absences . . . truants sometimes . . . a lot . . . stays away to help parents . . . makes illness an excuse.

2. SCHOOL WORK

Works steadily . . . works only when watched . . . inattentive . . . won't sit still . . . doesn't bother to learn . . . easily distracted . . . dreamy most of the time.

3. CLASSROOM STANDARD

(*a*) Working with own age group . . . year younger . . . year older.

(*b*) How does he compare with the rest of the children (position in class approximately).
Reading . . . good . . . average . . . poor for age . . . cannot read.
Arithmetic . . . good . . . average . . . poor for age . . . completely incompetent.

(*c*) Rate of progress . . . normal . . . late to start . . . going on well now . . . standing still.

4. ANY SPECIFIC DIFFICULTIES

(*a*) What?

(*b*) Possible causes—frequent changes of teacher . . . illness.

* I am indebted to psychologist colleagues who co-operated so willingly to helping in this way.

(c) Any extra help available?

Is he/she receiving extra help?
What?
How often?
For how long?

5. GAMES

Is he good at games? Yes . . . No—fools around . . . poor co-ordination.

6. CLASSROOM BEHAVIOUR

Well behaved . . . sometimes naughty . . . very naughty . . . hard to discipline . . . constantly needs petty correction.

7. ATTITUDE TO TEACHERS

Friendly . . . anxious to please . . . unfriendly . . . hostile.

8. COMPANIONSHIP

Good mixer . . . one or two friends only . . . likes to be the centre of attention . . . gets on well with other children . . . liked by other children . . . disliked . . . "buys friends" . . . seeks out younger children . . . always on fringe.

9. PARENTS' ATTITUDE

Co-operative and interested . . . disinterested . . . over-anxious.

10. Is teacher aware of anything of interest on Medical Card and its implications.

ADDITIONAL COMMENTS

In the "Additional Comments" the psychologist added his own judgement of the quality of the school and the teaching in relationship to the particular child attending there.

With the exception of children living in Cornwall and Wiltshire, as far as possible the children were tested at the hospitals in which the original study was based, i.e. St. Luke's Hospital, Guildford and Guy's Hospital, London. Because of the difficulty of transport for the parents, two Guildford children and one Guy's child were tested in their own homes. Every school except one was visited by a research assistant. The Guildford boy whose school was not visited, at the request of the parents, was a "Case." He was attending a private preparatory school in the town and was doing well. His parents did not wish the school to know of his previous history, nor did they wish him to attend hospital as they felt that also might upset the boy. He was, therefore, assessed at home and as much relevant information about the school and the home background was obtained from the parents on visiting the home.

For all the children who were tested at hospital, it was possible also to have a long interview with the mother or quite often father also came with the child so that it was possible to gain considerable information about the course of the child's developmental history during the period between the original and follow-up interviews with the child.

After considerable experimentation with various tests the following battery was chosen:

To assess overall general level of intellectual functioning the shortened form of the Wechsler Intelligence Scale for Children using two verbal and two performance items:

W.I.S.C.—Similarities
Vocabulary
Block design
Object assembly
Raven's Coloured Progressive Matrices Test

This non-verbal test was chosen with the purpose of identifying children who have good reasoning ability, but are below standard in verbal development and educational attainments.

To assess basic attainments the Sentence Reading Test–S.R.A. and the Neale Analysis of Reading Ability were used. The S.R.A. involves reading an incomplete sentence and underlining the word, chosen from a group of words, which best completes the sentence. This was carried out during the first testing period. The Neale Test was given separately one month later.

To assess understanding of number concepts and level of attainment in basic rules of Arithmetic, a test of "Computational Skill" was used.*

Of the 44 Cases assessed during the pre-school period 42 were traced for the follow-up. Of the original 63 Controls, 43 children were traced and used as Controls to this sample. It had been hoped to see all the children at ages 8 and 9, but many of them were difficult to trace. In much of the area round Guy's Hospital, slum property had been demolished and families rehoused. The time taken in tracing some of the children inevitably widened the spread of age range by the time it was possible to take them in to the follow-up study.

All the children, however, were still in their Primary Schools and, with few exceptions, were mainly 9 and 10 years of age.

Of the Cases, four were severely sub-normal and attended Training Centres, one was attending a school for "Educationally Sub-Normal" children and one girl was attending a school for physically handicapped children and although she had not sufficient use and control of her hands to do the Performance Scale of the W.I.S.C., she made a verbal I.Q. score of 85 and a Grade II, above average, score on the Coloured Matrices and Grade V (ages 4 to 7 years) in the Computational Skill Test.

From an examination of the test results, of the 42 Cases, four were severely sub-normal and made no scores on any of the tests used in this battery. One boy was educationally sub-normal and made no score on the reading tests. The physically handicapped

---

*This test item was being used experimentally in Manchester in the construction of the new British Intelligence Scale. It was made available for use here by courtesy of Mr. T. F. Fitzpatrick, acting director of the Manchester Research Team.

girl attending a P.H. school had not begun reading. Six other cases, five boys and one girl made no scores on the Reading Tests.

Six other boy Cases had reading ages on the Neale Test of at least 2 years below their chronological ages. Four other girl Cases had reading ages at least 2 years below their chronological ages. Two other girl Cases scored more than 2 years below their chronological ages on the Comprehension test of the Neale.

The picture is different in relation to the Arithmetical Computation test. Of all the children only two boys—both non-readers—made no score. All the girls and the other boy Cases, with, of course, the exception of the four severely sub-normal untestable children, made a score on this test. Many scored much below what might be expected in relation to their chronological ages.

The Mean and Standard Deviation of the scores is shown on Table 1. In Tables 2 and 3 the scores of the Younger and Older Boy and Girl Controls are shown separately and Tables 4 and 5 give the separate scores for Younger and Older Boy and Girl Cases. Table 6 gives the Mean and Standard Deviation of the scores of the 37 Cases which include the children who did not score on the Neale Reading Test.

An examination of the results obtained from this follow-up shows that five of the original Cases are globally damaged and functioning at a severely sub-normal or educationally sub-normal level. These children were easily identifiable at the pre-school assessment. The one severely physically handicapped child, though still a non-reader, is functioning well if one makes allowance for her handicap and her frequent school absences. Of the remaining 37 children, 7 girls and 11 boys were either non-readers or were reading at 28 months below the level of reading attainment which could be expected from their I.Q. levels (Yule, 1967). The procedure adopted for making a distinction between reading backwardness and reading retardation using Yule's formula is described fully in the Isle of Wight study. This was applicable only to the older groups. (Rutter, Tizard and

TABLE 1. CASES v. CONTROLS

	All Cases (31)		All Controls (43)	
	Mean	S.D.	Mean	S.D.
1. Age (first test)	44·58	8·37	43·74	6·47
2. Social Class	3·32	1·08	3·26	1·11
3. Reynell—Comp.	39·29	9·03	42·81	8·77
4. Reynell—Exp.	39·32	12·17	43·86	9·65
5. Form Copying	22·94	19·16	25·79	20·03
6. Block Concepts	16·68	6·26	18·30	5·33
7. Age at follow-up	112·23	18·65	112·58	18·36
8. W.I.S.C.—Sim.	11·61	3·17	13·23	2·93
9. W.I.S.C.—Voc.	12·06	2·78	13·09	2·73
10. W.I.S.C.—B.D.	12·10	3·07	13·19	3·19
11. W.I.S.C.—O.A.	12·13	3·17	12·30	3·54
12. Verbal Factor I.Q.	110·39	15·57	118·07	14·45
13. Performance Factor I.Q.	112·29	14·29	115·33	17·11
14. Full Scale I.Q.	109·23	11·25	113·81	11·91
15. Matrices—Raw	24·06	6·10	25·98	6·45
16. Matrices—Grade	2·71	0·97	2·51	0·80
17. Arithmetic—Raw	23·26	9·96	24·51	10·71
18. Arithmetic—Grade	3·16	1·19	3·37	1·22
19. S.R.A.—Raw	19·61	11·81	22·72	13·72
20. S.R.A.—Conv.	99·03	15·30	103·86	16·64
21. Neale—Acc.	105·16	16·95	115·74	21·69
22. Neale—Comp.	102·16	19·37	113·63	24·44

_N.B._—4 Cases were completely untestable at follow-up and a further 7 Cases were not scoring on the reading tests. This has the effect of inflating the average reading age of the Cases.

Whitmore, 1970). Using this estimate, most of the Cases and 14 of the Controls in the older groups were slightly underachieving, but none of the severity to regard them as having a specific reading disability. It is to this group of 18 children that we must look for evidence of identification in the test results of the pre-

TABLE 2. CONTROLS, BOYS

	Younger (12)		Older (12)		All (24)	
	Mean	S.D.	Mean	S.D.	Mean	S.D.
1. Age	38·33	2·67	48·50	1·57	43·42	5·62
2. Social Class	3·50	1·57	2·83	0·58	3·17	1·20
3. Reynell—Comp.	40·67	7·61	45·58	4·40	43·13	6·58
4. Reynell—Exp.	39·08	7·59	49·00	5·88	44·04	8·35
5. Form Copying	8·75	9·41	42·42	12·59	25·58	20·34
6. Block Concepts	15·08	6·14	21·33	3·45	18·21	5·82
7. Age (F./U.)	95·00	9·34	130·92	3·48	112·96	19·60
8. W.I.S.C.—Sim.	13·58	3·15	15·25	1·60	14·42	2·59
9. W.I.S.C.—Voc.	13·83	2·72	14·17	3·10	14·00	2·86
10. W.I.S.C.—B.D.	13·00	3·36	16·42	2·02	14·71	3·22
11. W.I.S.C.—O.A.	12·00	3·57	15·08	3·09	13·54	3·62
12. Verbal I.Q.	122·08	16·27	126·17	11·46	124·13	13·92
13. Performance I.Q.	114·33	18·82	132·25	9·86	123·29	17·31
14. Full Scale I.Q.	120·00	17·46	132·33	9·55	126·17	15·13
15. Matrices—Raw	23·25	5·40	32·00	2·13	27·63	6·01
16. Matrices—Grade	2·58	0·79	2·17	0·58	2·38	0·71
17. Arith.—Raw	17·08	6·24	34·83	6·98	25·96	11·14
18. Arith.—Grade	4·25	0·75	2·17	0·72	3·21	1·28
19. S.R.A.—Raw	14·83	9·33	32·83	8·65	23·83	12·73
20. S.R.A.—Conv.	103·08	16·01	111·25	18·05	107·17	17·20
21. Neale—Acc.	103·50	15·72	139·00	7·89	121·25	21·83
22. Neale—Comp.	104·33	23·15	137·50	9·65	120·92	24·24

school study.

The quality and method of class-room teaching, as well as the competence and personality of the teacher undoubtedly influences children's learning. It was quite outside the scope of this present follow-up study to make an adequate quantitative analysis of these important variables, but the information gathered from the school reports threw useful light on some of the factors which might have influenced the child's level of attainment.

TABLE 3. CONTROLS, GIRLS

	Younger (10)		Older (9)		All (19)	
	Mean	S.D.	Mean	S.D.	Mean	S.D.
1. Age	37·80	2·53	51·22	3·77	44·16	7·54
2. Social Class	4·10	0·57	2·56	0·73	3·69	1·01
3. Reynell—Comp.	36·40	11·85	49·11	5·01	42·42	11·13
4. Reynell—Exp.	35·70	8·37	52·44	6·56	43·63	11·31
5. Form Copying	9·00	7·27	45·00	9·50	26·05	20·19
6. Block Concepts	16·10	4·20	21·00	4·18	18·42	4·79
7. Age (F./U.)	96·70	5·19	129·22	2·73	112·11	17·18
8. W.I.S.C.—Sim.	10·80	3·05	12·78	1·86	11·74	2·68
9. W.I.S.C.—Voc.	11·20	2·66	12·78	0·83	11·95	2·12
10. W.I.S.C.—B.D.	10·40	1·78	12·22	1·48	11·26	1·85
11. W.I.S.C.—O.A.	10.20	2·57	11·33	3·08	10·74	2·81
12. Verbal I.Q.	105·90	13·35	115·44	5·94	110·42	11·34
13. Performance I.Q.	101·40	7·89	109·56	11·64	105·26	10·43
14. Full Scale I.Q.	104·10	9.71	113·89	8.77	108·74	10·32
15. Matrices—Raw	18·00	1·94	30·44	0·73	23·89	6·55
16. Matrices—Grade	3·30	0·82	2·00	0·00	2·68	0·89
17. Arith.—Raw	15·10	6·71	31·11	5·35	22·68	10·13
18. Arith.—Grade	4·40	0·84	2·67	0·50	3·58	1·12
19. S.R.A.—Raw	10·00	4·71	33·89	12·30	21·32	15·12
20. S.R.A.—Conv.	90·50	8·05	109·89	15·31	99·68	15·34
21. Neale—Acc.	93·30	11·10	126·00	11·09	108·79	19·94
22. Neale—Comp.	87·60	10·99	123·11	14·25	104·42	21·97

Of the 18 children:

Eight were having extra reading help at school, mainly short periods twice or three times a week from a peripatetic teacher trained in remedial work. Two of the children, twins, had been moved to a private school where they received very intensive individual help and had extra coaching during school holidays. One girl in the group had a quite severe hearing loss which had not been picked up till she was $6\frac{1}{2}$ years of age and failing badly

TABLE 4. CASES, BOYS

Variable	Younger (6)		Older (8)		All (14)	
	Mean	S.D.	Mean	S.D.	Mean	S.D.
1. Age First Test	35·83	0·75	52·63	0·74	45·43	8·65
2. Social Class	3·33	1·21	2·63	0·92	2·93	1·07
3. Reynell—Comp.	32·00	7·13	41·00	8·32	37·14	8·84
4. Reynell—Exp.	27·50	15·32	45·13	6·81	37·57	14·04
5. Form Copying	4·00	4·52	41·00	10·46	25·14	20·68
6. Block Concepts	13·17	4·12	20·25	3·15	17·21	5·01
7. Age—Follow-up	101·33	7·74	129·50	3·12	117·43	15·41
8. W.I.S.C.—Sim.	12·50	3·67	13·25	2·19	12·93	2·81
9. W.I.S.C.—Voc.	13·17	2·86	12·38	3·34	12·71	3·05
10. W.I.S.C.—B.D.	12·83	3·13	11·50	4·21	12·07	3·71
11. W.I.S.C.—O.A.	11·83	3·82	13·63	3·02	12·86	3·37
12. Verbal I.Q.	116·67	17·55	115·50	13·61	116·00	14·78
13. Performance I.Q.	113·33	19·45	115·00	17·65	114·29	17·72
14. Full Scale I.Q.	116·67	17·87	117·50	14·71	117·14	15·48
15. Matrices—Raw	23·67	3·72	28·50	5·10	26·43	5·05
16. Matrices—Grade	2·33	1·03	2·75	1·17	2·57	1·09
17. Arith.—Raw	22·17	6·24	26·63	9·01	24·71	7·99
18. Arith.—Grade	3·33	0·82	2·75	1·04	3·00	0·96
19. S.R.A.—Raw	15·50	5·68	26·50	11·83	21·79	10·94
20. S.R.A.—Conv.	97·83	13·12	101·13	21·92	99·71	18·11
21. Neale—Acc.	97·67	15·21	111·38	19·35	105·50	18·44
22. Neale—Comp.	96·33	20·53	109·13	20·50	103·64	20·78

at school. By the time of this follow-up study, this girl had come under the care of the hospital otologist and was receiving extra reading help from a teacher who had also had much experience as a teacher of the deaf.

Three of the children in the group were having speech therapy. In two other cases, their teacher had remarked on the frequent absences and lack of "caring" on the part of the parents. One girl was In Care during the time of the early study. She had been

TABLE 5. CASES, GIRLS

	Younger (10)		Older (7)		All (17)	
	Mean	S.D.	Mean	S.D.	Mean	S.D.
1. Age	37·40	1·96	53·14	3·02	43·88	8·33
2. Social Class	4·20	0·42	2·86	1·07	3·65	1·00
3. Reynell—Comp.	39·10	10·99	43·86	4·67	41·06	9·05
4. Reynell—Exp.	36·80	11·71	46·43	5·62	40·76	10·62
5. Form Copying	8·50	6·90	39·14	13·11	21·12	18·24
6. Block Concepts	12·40	6·57	21·71	4·03	16·24	7·26
7. Age (F./U.)	92·00	5·12	130·71	6·47	107·94	20·40
8. W.I.S.C.—Sim.	10·10	3·25	11·14	3·02	10·53	3·10
9. W.I.S.C.—Voc.	11·60	2·84	11·43	2·15	11·53	2·50
10. W.I.S.C.—B.D.	11·30	1·64	13·29	3·25	12·12	2·55
11. W.I.S.C.—O.A.	11·10	2·81	12·14	3·29	11·53	2·96
12. Verbal I.Q.	105·00	16·47	106·86	13·99	105·76	15·06
13. Performance I.Q.	107·50	10·87	115·14	10·32	110·65	11·02
14. Full Scale I.Q.	107·10	13·90	111·71	12·50	109·00	13·14
15. Matrices—Raw	17·90	2·81	28·14	4·81	22·12	6·33
16. Matrices—Grade	2·90	0·88	2·71	0·95	2·82	0·88
17. Arith.—Raw	15·10	7·08	32·00	8·78	22·06	11·43
18. Arith.—Grade	4·00	1·15	2·29	0·95	3·29	1·36
19. S.R.A.—Raw	10·20	7·67	28·71	9·74	17·82	12·53
20. S.R.A.—Conv.	97·20	10·80	100·29	16·65	98·47	13·12
21. Neale—Acc.	95·60	13·16	118·14	9·49	104·88	16·19
22. Neale—Comp.	90·40	15·47	116·00	11·20	100·94	18·69

in and out of hospital as a battered child. When she was seen at the follow-up, her parents had separated and she was living at home with her mother, but though the hospital staff knew this child well in her pre-school years, it was not easy to get a very clear picture of her history since she had started school and lived at home. She was described at school as one of their very deprived children from a home impoverished materially and also limited

TABLE 6. 37 CASES (INCLUDING 6 WITH NO NEALE RESULTS)

	Mean	S.D.	T—Tests—Cases v. Controls 31 v. 43	37 v. 43
1. Age	43·68	8.06	—	—
2. Social Class	3·43	1·07	—	—
3. Reynell Comp.	36·22	11·32	1·68	2·93**
4. Expression	36·24	13·72	1·79	2·90
5. Form Copying	19·38	19·32	0·61	1·45
6. Block Concepts	15·32	6·90	1·20	2·18*
7. Age (F./U.)	109·46	18·26	—	—
8. W.I.S.C.—Sim.	10·81	3·59	2·27*	3·32**
9. W.I.S.C.—Voc.	11·35	3·18	1·59	2·63*
10. W.I.S.C.—B.D.	11·16	3·85	1·47	2·58*
11. W.I.S.C.—O.A.	11·30	3·60	0·21	1·25
12. Verbal I.Q.	106·00	18·38	2·18*	3·29**
13. Performance I.Q.	107·19	18·60	0·81	2·04*
14. Full Scale I.Q.	105·27	14·49	1·67	2·89**
15. Matrices—Raw	22·76	6·51	1·29	2·22*
16. Matrices—Grade	2·86	1·00	0·97	1·74
17. Arith.—Raw	20·51	11·32	0·51	1·62
18. Arith.—Grade	3·46	1·28	0·74	0·32
19. S.R.A.—Raw	16·43	13·04	1·02	2·09*
20. S.R.A. Conv.	—	—	1·27	—
21. Neale—Acc.	—	—	2·26*	—
22. Neale—Comp.	—	—	2·17*	—

* = Significant at 5% level.
** = Significant at 1% level.

N.B.—Comparing the 37 cases with the 43 controls, they were significantly poorer on three of four tests given originally (Nos. 3–6), and continue to be poor on *verbal* items at follow-up. Overall they are significantly poorer on reading as measured by the group test (raw score). Six of the cases were so poor that they were totally unable to read. Even after excluding these six from the calculations, the remaining 31 are still significantly lower on all the reading tests than the controls.

in its capacity for giving emotional support and care to this child. She was said to have been very late in beginning to speak and also nutritionally impoverished, but in the follow-up interview with the mother, she, herself an unhappy and depressed woman, could tell us little.

One of the brightest boys among the Cases who had not made a beginning in reading, was emotionally maladjusted and was attending the local Child Guidance Clinic for treatment. This took him out of school for two half-days a week. One boy had had meningitis which caused a long absence from school at age $6\frac{3}{4}$ years and considerable difficulty in adjusting to school on his return.

It can be seen from this brief record that there are many varied factors difficult to quantify but which inevitably make a valuable contribution towards influencing the child's success or failure in school.

In their discussion of plans for predicting the children who are possibly at risk of having difficulties in learning to read, Jansky and de Hirsch (1972) list the following factors noticed during the kindergarten period which would contribute to the reliability of the predictions:

1. A positive attitude on the part of the parents towards education in relation to their children.
2. Regularity of the child's attendance at school.
3. The ability to concentrate on his own individual work.
4. Capacity for independent work.
5. Persistence in spite of frustrations.
6. Capacity for attention and listening.
7. Good use of oral language.
8. Interest in books and reading.
9. The child's own desire to read.

These writers strongly hold that a subjective assessment based on the above factors and made often almost intuitively by the kindergarten teacher should be combined with objective data in the attempt to construct a screening test procedure which would reliably identify children who are likely to fail in learning to read when they reach the age of formal schooling.

In the early study here described in Chapter 3, the child's concentration and freedom from distractibility, his independence and his capacity to co-operate were all rated from observation during the test period in the belief that the neurologically damaged child often lacked these abilities. While poor functioning in these areas of behaviour inevitably contribute to school failure, it is difficult to assess the extent to which these factors create a specific reading failure rather than total lowered educational achievement.

Observation of the children's performance during the study of pre-school children emphasised for this writer the primary importance of language development in its contribution to school learning in all areas of achievement.

The correlations between the Reynell Reading scores (tested at the pre-school level) and the scores on the W.I.S.C. and the Matrices used at follow-up as measures of intellectual functioning is shown on Table 7. It is interesting that the correlations in the Control group between Reynell's Verbal ability scores are significantly lower than that of the group of Cases.

TABLE 7. 37 CASES

	V.F. I.Q.	P.F. I.Q.	F.S. I.Q.	Matrices
Neale—Acc.	0·52	0·52	0·57	0·57
Neale—Comp.	0·63	0·59	0·67	0·61
Neale—S.R.A.	0·65	0·64	0·68	0·73
Arith. (Raw)	0·68	0·75	0·75	0·74
Reynell—Comp.	0·44	0·57	0·53	0·43
Reynell—Expr.	0·45	0·55	0·52	0·48

The correlations between the Neale reading test results and scores on early test results are shown on Table 8. There seems here a marked difference between the correlations of the group of 31 Cases and the Control group between Form copying at 4

TABLE 8. CONTROLS' RESULTS SHOWING THE CORRELATIONS BETWEEN
EARLY RESULTS AND NEALE READING

	NEALE	
	Accuracy	Comprehension
Reynell—Comprehension	0·37	0·39
Reynell—Expression	0·57	0·55
Form Copying	0·76	0·71
Block Concepts	0·54	0·55

IN THE 31 CASES, A DIFFERENT PICTURE EMERGES:

	NEALE	
	Accuracy	Comprehension
Reynell—Comprehension	0·46	0·47
Reynell—Expression	0·61	0·62
Form Copying	0·51	0·45
Block Concepts	0·51	0·62

years and the Neale scores at the follow-up period, but the
differences fall just short of the 5% level of significance. During
the testing period of the pre-school children, striking characteristics were noticed in the children's mode of carrying out the
non-verbal tests. It was clear that most of the children who
scored well used verbalizing as a tool of their thinking in a way
which was not demonstrated in their carrying out the Reynell
test. Form copying is essentially a perceptuo-motor task but it
has been shown by many, as for example by Luria (1961) that
visual discrimination demonstrated in perceptuo-motor tasks can
be helped by using language as an aid to performing the task in
hand.

Writing of the contribution of perceptuo-motor skills to
educational adequacy, Wedell (1973) shows how "language
facility is likely to help children to learn to discriminate those
visual features relevant to reading".

In order to combine the various developing abilities so that they are brought to the aid of performance in different tasks, a child needs to be able to integrate these various skills and from observation of the ways in which these children carry out their various school tasks, their success in achievement depends greatly on their ability to integrate information derived from one type of sense modality with another. Observation of the children who were chosen from the Cases for their reading disability in the follow-up study would seem to confirm that they are seriously handicapped in their ability to integrate information derived from one sense modality to others.

The patients were selected in the newborn period because of major problems for instance, serious problems in delivery, absence or asymmetry of primitive responses, hypotonia, cyanotic attack, focal fits, abnormally persistent fisting and apathy, premature birth and small for dates babies.

It is of interest that when this group was followed up a high frequency of abnormality was later discovered. The purpose of the study was to compare the functioning of these children at age 4 and at 8 or 9 and to assess the predictive value of the findings at age 4. The follow-up results confirm the predictive value in the results of the original study (page 57).

Although this study as at present constructed was not intended to show the predictive value of abnormalities in the newborn period, it is not without significance that of the children who showed clear specific learning disabilities, particularly in reading failure at follow-up, none were in the "Control" group. Of the "Cases" there were 18 children with severe specific reading difficulty. Of the 37 cases who fell within the normal range of overall I.Q., 19 had gone through early schooling without showing any evidence of difficulty, but 18 of the children were presenting severe specific learning disabilities, especially in reading.

Except for the children severely damaged in the neonatal period and consequently functioning globally at an educationally sub-normal level, it has not been possible to ascertain why some of the remaining Cases had quite marked specific disabilities while others managed in school to function evenly in relation to their intelligence level. These children have been able to compensate for their neurological dysfunction by drawing on other undamaged areas of the brain.*

This follow-up study raises many questions that remain unanswered, but it is clear that children who suffer certain kinds of neurological damage at birth even though very mild can develop specific learning disorders which demand special remedial intervention in order to help them to overcome their difficulties. The kind of approach to helping them is not the same for every child, but the good teacher is one who can adjust the pattern of remediation helped by her own observation and the understanding of the problems of the individual child in a team approach with the paediatricians and psychologists who can contribute to the different facets needed in understanding the child and his problems.

*The author is in process of writing a formal paper giving a more detailed account of an analysis of these problems.

Historical Survey

AN UNDERSTANDING of the course of research into specific learning difficulties is essential to the planning of suitable methods of treatment. What follows here is purely an historical survey. A critical assessment of some of the work done has been made earlier in the study where relevant.

Research of a major character began in America. It was there that the classical pioneer work of Strauss (1947) and his colleagues took place. However, even before this there were a number of publications by workers in various aspects of this field that are worthy of note.

Writing of developmental diagnosis, Gesell and Amatruda (1941) devoted a section of their chapter on Cerebral Injury to a discussion of minimal injury. In this section, the authors describe what they call "a sizeable group of cases which presented atypical syndromes that could only be accounted for on the basis of mild or resolving injury". They go on to describe how the diagnosis of minimal cerebral injury is not always supported by the birth history and neo-natal history, but they stress the importance of taking into account the total behavioural picture, while reserving the diagnosis of minimal injury to those cases in which the symptoms have a definite neurological import. Describing the developmental manifestations of minimal injury, they show how the synergy and smoothness of all motor co-ordinations are affected in many of these cases so that there is evidence of inco-ordination in gross as well as in fine motor behaviour. Many of their cases had in early infancy shown difficulty in sucking, which in the pre-school period asserted itself in a tendency to stutter. They found also a sizeable group of children with speech defects, poorly defined lateral dominance and delayed integration, which later resulted in prevalence of reading disabilities. They emphasized also the mildly damaged child's need for more than ordinary protection from stress and competition, particularly during the early years. They concluded:

> In all these cases we are dealing with an extremely complicated interaction of developmental potentialities and dynamic forces. Even though the original motor injury was mild, the damages in the personality sphere may be considerable and more or less permanent. In the interpretation of the development of these infants, psychiatric concepts are often less helpful than an understanding of developmental neurology.

This whole chapter, with its sensitively portrayed illustrative case histories, merits careful re-reading. Even now, it presents a remarkably up-to-date picture of the diagnostic as well as the developmental problems still surrounding these syndromes.

It was in this same year that Goldstein and Scheerer (1941) published their monograph on *Abstract and Concrete Behaviour*. Although this is concerned primarily with the behavioural and cognitive difficulties of brain-injured adults, it contains much that is pertinent to the functioning of damaged children. At this time also Bender, working in Bellevue Hospital, New York, was showing considerable interest in and concern with the problems of brain disorders in children. In 1948, she published a paper on *Body Image Problems of the Brain Damaged Child* and in 1949, one on *Psychological Problems of Children with Organic Brain Disease*. Later (1959), she brought together her findings in book form.

Among others who must be regarded as forerunners in recognizing certain aspects of neurological handicap in children is Orton. As early as 1925, he called the attention of medical colleagues in neurology and psychiatry to the fact that many otherwise normal children have language problems, including among many a specific difficulty in learning to read. Orton had been trained as a neuropathologist and in his early work had been interested in adult aphasic patients who had suffered loss or impairment of their language function through injury to the brain. In his later work with school children, their difficulties in learning to read struck him as being similar to those of the adult patients, though the children differed fundamentally from the adults because they showed no evidence whatsoever of brain damage or of brain defects. These children seemed to have particular difficulty in remembering whole word patterns, the orientation of letters and the order of letters in words. He coined the word "strepho-symbolia" (twisted symbols) to describe their difficulty and he regarded this condition as a developmental delay, which he believed should yield to proper methods of teaching. Orton published a number of papers on the various aspects of this condition of "word-blindness" and later (1937) brought together his findings in his book *Reading, Writing and Speech Problems in Children*. This book remains a classic in the field of special language disorders in children.

The Work of Strauss and his Colleagues

The publication in 1947 of Strauss and Lehtinen's *Psychopathology and Education of the Brain Injured Child* is generally accepted as a landmark in the exploration of the characteristics of this "brain-injured child" syndrome. Writing in 1966, Clements describes it as "the first comprehensive presentation on the topic" and continues:

> few single volumes have been so influential in the production of fresh considerations in the areas of pathology, diagnosis, education and investigation of children with learning and behavioural disabilities. It refocused attention on the neglected area of individual differences among children. It also is an excellent illustration of the usefulness of collaboration on a problem area.

In 1955, Strauss in collaboration with Kephart published a second volume—*The Brain-Injured Child—Progress in Theory and Clinic*.

Volume I is based on some 20 years of research and work with brain-injured children, whom they describe as follows:

> a brain-injured child is a child who before, during or after birth has received an injury to or suffered an infection of the brain. As a result of

such organic impairment, defects of the neuro-motor system may be present or absent; however, such a child may show disturbances in perception, thinking and emotional behaviour either separately or in combination. These disturbances can be demonstrated by specific tests. These disturbances prevent or impede a normal learning process.

One of the important contributions by Strauss at this time is his distinction between the "exogenous" and the "endogenous" retarded child. He classified the endogenous group of children as those for whom there was no history of perinatal or later childhood nervous system damage. In the children of the exogenous group, there was a history of such risk of insult to the central nervous system. Comparison of the two groups showed that, despite some overlap, the children in the exogenous group showed more hyper-activity, were more perceptually disordered, more distractible and emotionally more labile than those in the endogenous group. It was to children showing these unusual patterns of behavioural organization that the term "brain-injured" came to be applied.

Strauss went on to show how this pattern, characteristic of the exogenous child, with disturbances in perception, concept formation and also in emotional behaviour, could occur in children whose overall intelligence was within the normal range. He showed how many of these disturbances in perception and thinking and language could be demonstrated by special tests, which he described. He also showed how children with exogenous retardation could be differentiated from children with more general mental retardation due to endogenous or familial factors. It was Strauss who first stressed the difficulty in figure–ground discrimination experienced by many of these brain-injured children. It was to this that he attributed the cause for their hyperactive behaviour and distractibility. In the second part of the book, Lehtinen presents general principles in the education of these children and suggests ways by which their hyperactivity and distractibility can be reduced, particularly during times of school learning.

In Volume II (1955), *Progress in Theory and Clinic*, Strauss and Kephart sought to present more up-to-date views on brain functioning, as new data had accumulated. In this book they are concerned with "the clinical syndrome of the brain-injured child who is not mentally defective but who in spite of 'normalcy in I.Q.' as tested is still 'defective' ". Their aim is to extend their theoretical understanding of brain injury in children, in the hope that this will lead to a more effective treatment and education of so-called "normal" brain-injured children.

The demonstration of diagnostic procedures and special educational methods applied to these children in the Cove Schools at Racine and Evanston aroused great interest in the United States. The main deviations characteristic of these children lie in disturbances in perception, poor motor co-ordination, language disorders, difficulties in concept formation and disturbances in behaviour, mainly seen in hyperactivity, distractibility and fluctuation of mood.

From the viewpoint of the educationist, these children clearly need special educational provision. In the United States, as well as in this country, attempts are being made to provide suitable teaching programmes. These various educational provisions will be discussed later.

Perceptual and Visuo-spatial Disorders

The understanding of visuo-spatial and perceptual problems has aroused the interest of psychologists, and many limited, but pertinent studies in this field have been published. Although primarily concerned with perceptual and visuo-motor disorders in cerebral palsy, Abercrombie's (1964) extensive review of this field of study is equally relevant to other children with specific learning difficulties arising from disorders of perception.

The neurological aspects of the condition of these possibly damaged children have also been the focus of considerable research study. Knobloch and Pasamanick (1959 and 1960) have devoted much intensive research study to factors emerging from their evaluations of deviations from normal neurological functioning in infancy. They hold that there is a continuum of damage, which ranges from minimal to severe, and that there is a close relationship between neurological integrity and maturational level. They have also demonstrated that children in whom events associated with brain injury have occurred in the neo-natal period show later learning disabilities and behaviour problems.

Writing of *Minimal Chronic Brain Syndromes in Children*, Richmond Paine (1962) describes forty-one children who were referred for neurological consultation because of poor school work, overactivity, clumsiness, poor speech or emotional problems and in whom there had been no previous definite diagnosis of neurological abnormality. Paine found that thirty-one of these children showed definite abnormal neurological signs and nine of the other ten were at least excessively clumsy. Paine suggests that there is a syndrome of minimal brain damage and that sub-clinical affections could exist in any of the four main areas in which function may be deranged by a chronic brain lesion, namely motor, intellectual, perceptual and convulsive.

Later, in collaboration with Oppé (1966) he published a detailed account of the *Neurological Examination of Children*, which provides useful information relevant to organic neurological impairment in children.

Under the editorship of Hellmuth (1965) Special Child Publications have in volume 1 on *Learning Disorders*, produced what is described by Doll as a "frontier volume" on learning processes. The first chapter of this volume by Paine on "Organic Neurological Factors Related to Learning Disorders", gives a clear and useful picture of this syndrome.

This "frontier volume" contains essays on various aspects of learning disorder, approached from many disciplines. An interesting chapter, "Motor Generalisations in Space and Time" by Dunsing and Kephart, presents very clearly the viewpoint of workers at the Achievement Center for Children in Purdue University, Indiana. Kephart is the Director of this Center. The chapter describes the principles on which his methods are based; these methods as applied in the classroom are explained in detail in his book *The Slow Learner in the Classroom* (1960). Another chapter in volume 1 which repays careful reading is by Johnson and Myklebust on "Dyslexia in Childhood". Myklebust is Professor of Language Pathology in Northwestern University, Illinois, and Johnson is Assistant Professor in the same department. It is not surprising, therefore, that they regard dyslexia as part of a basic language and learning disability. They hold that the reading process is an integral part of symbolic language and behaviour and it is from this point of view that they discuss diagnosis and methods of remedial teaching. They believe that if we are to understand this condition properly, we need to understand the ways by which a person learns to symbolize experience.

Developmental Neurology

Two further volumes in this series have now been published— vol. 2 (1964) and vol. 3 (1968) and it is interesting to note the increasing emphasis, particularly in the latter volume, on "developmental neurology" and the need for psychologists to have also a basic neurological training in order to work as "neuro-psychologists".

Characteristic of this approach is Marion Stuart's (1963) *Neurophysiological Insights into Teaching*. The aim of this book is to present methods of teaching children who have specific language difficulties in reading, writing and spelling. In it Stuart seeks to link the art of teaching with the science of the study of the human organism, or, as she describes it, to bring a "neurophysiological approach to the understanding of the learning behaviours of children". This is essentially a book by a highly intelligent teacher for teachers. The author draws on relevant research studies in her presentation of a neurological approach to learning. She re-emphasizes the importance of recognizing individual differences in children's ways of learning and—equally important —the need to assess the successful outcome for the individual child of any teaching method employed.

In 1967 Paine reported on a review of ninety children who were seen as patients in the Children's Hospital, Washington, D.C., during the past 3 years. These children were a heterogeneous group, suffering from various combinations, in varying proportions, of minor motor disabilities and "soft neurological signs", perceptual impairment, disproportionate difficulty in abstract thought and in tasks involving visual motor co-ordination, various behavioural characteristics, many cases also showed E.E.G. abnormalities. A complete matrix of cross-correlations was calculated in relation to histories of potential cerebral insults in the pre-natal, perinatal and post-natal periods. Certain combinations of signs and symptoms stood out as having a greater or lesser correlation with abnormal objective neurological signs on examination or with E.E.G. abnormalities.

Since only about 50 per cent of the children had histories of any past recognizable potential cerebral insult, Paine suggests that those children in whom an association with histories of potential causes of brain damage is lacking may have had cerebral insults not recognizable in our present state of knowledge, or may reflect irregular maturation of cerebral function of a nature as yet unexplained.

Communication Disorders in Brain-damaged Children

In a discussion of *Communication Disorders in Brain-Damaged Children*, Pond (1967), who has always tended to emphasize the possibility that many learning disorders could be directly due to psychiatric disturbances in children, suggests that speech is one of the best examples of "species–specific signals that does not get developed unless the earliest stages of the child's relationships are smooth enough to pave the way for the exploration of the 'Other' outside". He stresses that:

the learning problem is not just the acquisition of motor skills and perceptual patterns, but, in the structuring of the inner world of the child's mind which is not a *tabula rasa*, but a mass of seething and contradictory forces and fantasies. Because learning to read and write involves organising perceptual experiences and motor responses in various differing fields, the child needs to be equipped with the necessary motor and perceptual skills, which may be interfered with by bodily disturbances or brain lesions but the main learning process consists of the cutting out of irrelevant responses at the psychological as well as the physiological level.

Because the child has to use language for the expression of his own feelings and in doing so has to learn to inhibit inappropriate feelings and fantasies, it is not surprising that learning the techniques of communication often becomes the focus of emotional disorders and so distorts and blocks the learning process. Pond holds that "the contribution to the aetiological problem can go no further at the present time than the general formulation that there may be an underlying disturbance in maturation which can manifest itself in a large number of ways". Nevertheless, he does not rule out the possible influence of neurophysiological disturbance, but he believes that the presence of definite brain lesions seems neither necessary nor sufficient, "though the occurrence of such lesions in children with specific learning difficulties may be greater than by chance. . . . The underlying neurological disorder, if any, in children with these specific defects, seems to partake of the nature of a constitutional immaturity leading to dyssymbolia".

The Choreiform Syndrome

Prechtl's work in Gröningen is also relevant to the study of minimal brain damage. He describes what he named the choreiform syndrome (1962) and suggests that children identified by neurological examination in early infancy as showing this syndrome later develop more than normal difficulties in learning, and particularly in reading.

Nooteboom (1968) also suggests that a choreatiform syndrome is a cause of some learning and behaviour difficulties in children whose developmental processes have been disturbed from birth by pre-natal, para-natal or post-natal hypoxia. She suggests that these children can be identified by a careful analysis of some psychological tests. But this work is still in a research stage.

Clumsy Children

Much of the interest in Britain in children thought to have organic neurological impairment has arisen from increased recognition of the learning difficulties of various categories of cerebral palsied children. Walton *et al.* (1962, 1963 and 1965) working in Newcastle, and Gordon (1966) in Manchester have made careful case studies of children whom they describe as "clumsy" children. They suggest that though some of these children have added difficulties in visuo-spatial perception and concept formation, various types of apraxia and agnosia of congenital origin or arising in infancy can occur in isolation. They present interesting case studies and suggest that the syndrome of clumsiness due to developmental apraxia and agnosia is not uncommon and can easily be overlooked. The diagnostic and educational problems which such children present are vividly described. In his account of *The Normal School Child* (1964) Illingworth described in some detail "clumsy" children as showing many of the disabilities in some ways similar to those seen in adults with parietal lobe damage and described as "Gerstmann's Syndrome". Left to struggle with the demands of a normal school, they frequently develop an overlay of emotional disturbance and react badly to stress. Illingworth suggests that these are cases of "minimal cerebral palsy".

Recognizing the need to clarify some of these concepts, reports of conferences on particular themes related to the field of organic impairment are of interest.

In 1962, the third international study group under the auspices of the English Spastics' Society held at Oxford took as its theme "Minimal Cerebral Dysfunction". The proceedings of this multi-disciplinary group are published under that title. Much time was given during that conference to discussion of terminology. It was felt that the term "minimal brain damage" was loaded with too many diverse meanings. Sometimes, it is linked to a behaviour syndrome attributed to brain damage, sometimes to peculiar intellectual dysfunctions and sometimes to motor disorders. It was generally agreed that the term "minimal brain damage" should be abandoned. Although the concept of "minimal brain damage" had probably served a useful purpose in bringing together a number of hitherto unrecognized conditions, the group of children previously classified under this heading is heterogeneous and tends to disguise the need for more detailed diagnosis.

Further efforts to clarify the problems of brain damage in children are described in the report of a conference which was held at the Children's Hospital of Philadelphia in 1964. This conference, also multi-disciplinary, was mainly concerned with the social and educational management of these children, and the proceedings are published under the editorship of Birch. Again, there is some controversy regarding a definition of "brain-damaged" children and in this volume, Birch uses it to designate a behaviour pattern. He says:

> Despite the fact that "brain damage" is an unfortunate diagnostic label in that it implies both the existence of etiologic knowledge where none exists and a stereotyped view of the consequences of cerebral injury, there is little doubt that the children designated by it constitute an important clinical grouping. . . . The issue may for practical purposes be resolved if it is agreed that the entity with which we are concerned is not a neurologic designation but a behaviour pattern . . . . The category is entirely behavioural.

He implies that any of a number of kinds of cerebral damage will result in a common pattern of behavioural disturbance. In this pattern he includes disordered behaviour, short attention span, specific learning disorders and impulsive and restless behaviour.

Apart from the interest of the varying approaches of the participants, this book makes a start at a more precise analysis of what is meant by brain damage in children and what it involves for the child. There is also a most extensive bibliography of the literature up to date, with a valuable set of abstracts.

In January 1966, the first of a series of reports on *Minimal Brain Dysfunction in Children* was published by the Public Health Service of the U.S. Department of Health, Education and Welfare in Washington, D.C. This report is described as phase 1 of a three-phase project whose purpose, described by Masland, is: "to study the special medical and educational needs of that group of children whose dysfunction does not produce gross motor or sensory deficit or generalised impairment of intellect, but who exhibit limited alterations of behaviour or intellectual functioning".

This first report, *Task Force I*, written by the project director, Clements, is concerned with terminology and identification. He defines the "Minimal Brain Dysfunction Syndrome" as follows:

> The term "minimal brain dysfunction syndrome" refers in this paper to children of near average, average, or above average general intelligence with certain learning or behavioural disabilities ranging from mild to severe, which are associated with deviations of function of the central nervous system. These deviations may manifest themselves by various combinations of impairment in perception, conceptualisation, language, memory, and control of attention, impulse, or motor function.
>
> Similar symptoms may or may not complicate the problems of children with cerebral palsy, epilepsy, mental retardation, blindness, or deafness.
>
> These aberrations may arise from genetic variations, bio-chemical irregularities, perinatal brain insults, other illnesses or injuries sustained during the years which are critical for the development and maturation of the central nervous system, or from unknown causes.
>
> The definition also allows for the possibility that early severe sensory deprivation could result in central nervous system alterations, which may be permanent.
>
> During the school years, a variety of learning disabilities is the most prominent manifestation of the condition which can be designated by this term.
>
> The group of symptoms included under the term "minimal brain dysfunction" stems from disorders which may manifest themselves in severe form as a variety of well-recognized conditions. The child with minimal brain dysfunction may exhibit these minor symptoms in varying degree and in varying combinations.

Having reached some agreement regarding nomenclature, the report goes on to describe the symptoms by which these children can be identified. It bases these on the results of a review of some 100 recent publications. The descriptive elements culled from the literature are classified under the following headings:

Test Performance Indicators
Impairments of Perception and Concept-formation
Specific Neurologic Indicators

Disorders of Speech and Communication
Disorders of Motor Function
Academic Achievement and Adjustment
Disorders of Thinking Processes
Physical Characteristics
Emotional Characteristics
Sleep Characteristics
Relationship Capacities
Variations of Physical Development
Characteristics of Social Behaviour
Variations of Personality
Disorders of Attention and Concentration

Finally they extricate the ten characteristics most often cited by the various authors in order of frequency:

1. Hyperactivity.
2. Perceptual-motor impairments.
3. Emotional lability.
4. General co-ordination deficits.
5. Disorders of attention (short attention span, distractibility, perseveration).
6. Impulsivity.
7. Disorders of memory and thinking.
8. Specific learning disabilities: (a) reading, (b) arithmetic, (c) writing, (d) spelling.
9. Disorders of speech and hearing.
10. Equivocal neurological signs and electro-encephalo-graphic irregularities.

Clements then goes on to point out that certain symptoms tend to cluster to form recognizable clinical entities. As examples, he cites the "hyperkinetic syndrome" and the "hypokinetic syndrome" (in which primary reading retardation and some aphasias occur).

In the final section, diagnostic evaluation and criteria are briefly discussed and the difference is stressed between the objectives of the "medical" as opposed to the "educational" diagnosis. The objectives of the medical diagnosis are given as "to demonstrate the existence of any causative factors of disease or injury capable of amelioration or prevention", while the objective of the educational diagnosis is "to make possible the establishment of appropriate remedial programmes of management and education". Guidelines for the diagnostic evaluation of deviating children are then set out under the two categories—Medical Evaluation and Behavioural Assessment—in which psychological, language and educational evaluation are included.

The need for multi-disciplinary diagnostic programmes is emphasized. More detailed consideration of this need and the problems arising from it is the subject of further study by Task Force II, not yet published. A tentative report from the Educational Sub-committee of Task Force II has been finished, but also not yet published. The report of Task Force III is not yet completed.

Children with Language Disorders

Auditory Imperception or Central Deafness

In 1964, the report edited by Renfrew and Murphy of a Conference on "The Child Who does not Talk" was published and contains much that is relevant to those special learning disabilities which arise from language disorders. In this book, Gordon (1964) presents a useful account of the concept of central deafness or auditory imperception, which he defined as: "An abnormal response to auditory stimuli due to a disorder of function within the central nervous system proximal to the auditory nuclei in the brain stem." Gordon holds that this concept of central deafness is of practical importance because, particularly in the early years, a child who has "central deafness" may easily be mis-diagnosed as a child with peripheral deafness and could then be mistakenly educated as a peripherally deaf child—a type of educational programme which is not beneficial for the "centrally deaf" child.

Developmental Dyslexia

In 1962, the report of the proceedings of a Johns Hopkins Conference on Research Needs and Prospects in Dyslexia and Related Aphasic Disorders was published under the editorship of John Money. Representatives of many disciplines participated— paediatricians, neurologists, psychiatrists, psychologists, specialists in speech and hearing and educationists.

As would be expected in a multi-disciplinary conference on a subject which is even yet controversial, many disagreements emerged. Nevertheless, for those concerned with problems of special reading disabilities in children, the papers presented at the conference make interesting reading. Zangwill (1962), himself a participant, summarizes as follows the points on which reasonable agreement appeared to be reached:

1. Developmental dyslexia is to be regarded as endogenous and almost certainly arises on a neurological basis. It is not primarily a psychiatric disorder.
2. Dyslexia is seldom wholly specific: retarded speech, poor development of verbal skills and certain minor disorders of motor function are commonly found.
3. Defects of visual form perception are not essential correlates of developmental dyslexia.
4. Anomalies of laterality in dyslexics are perhaps less significant than was at one time supposed.
5. Remedial education is worth-while.

The whole concept of developmental dyslexia remains extremely controversial and ranges from the belief by Critchley (1961 and 1964) that it is a specific constitutional genetically determined disorder, which is distinguished from other forms of reading disability by "its gravity and purity", to the many teachers who regard it as falling at the extreme end of a continuum of children with reading disabilities. The case for this is made strongly by Rutter (1968) in his study of poor and backward readers in the school population of the Isle of Wight.

A recently published survey by Doehring (1969) and colleagues stresses the value of a neuropsychological approach to an understanding of specific reading disability, or developmental dyslexia, which they define as a severe impairment of reading acquisition in a child who appears to be otherwise normal. This study was carried out by a group of experienced neuropsychologists and the results tentatively present many further directions along which research into this complicated subject could usefully proceed.

Pre-school Children

To date, there has been comparatively little published work regarding pre-school children with possible neurological impairment. Two studies based on clinical experience are of interest here.

Working for many years with handicapped children in New York, Haeussermann (1956 and 1958) has built up a body of information for the clinical evaluation of behavioural functions in the brain-damaged or retarded child without motor handicaps. She describes the purpose of her procedure "not to produce a quantitative measurement of a child's level, although such a level becomes evident during the evaluation procedure. The aim is an inventory of the young child's developmental potential and of the intactness or lack of intactness of his pattern of functioning". Her aim is to relate her findings to plans for suitable education of the child so that in this way, much misery and defeat arising out of wrong experimentation and mistakes can be avoided.

Working at the Paediatric Language Disorder Clinic in New York, De Hirsch (1957) believed that it was possible to identify with some degree of accuracy the children at the 5–6 year age-level who are liable to have difficulty in the beginnings of learning to read. Most of her tests are designed to assess the child's level of maturation in the various areas of functioning. She has also stated that—"Clinical observation shows that it is possible to predict future dyslexics in a fairly large percentage of 3-, 4- and 5-year-olds who are originally referred on account of motor speech delay, developmental word-deafness and severe dyslalia."

Examination of motor, perceptual and emotional performance has shown:

> a number of basic and specific dysfunctions which seem to underlie a variety of language disturbances. These children frequently have difficulty in fine muscular control; some of them show a degree of dyspraxia. Many are late in establishing cerebral dominance and have trouble with right–left progression. Bender Gestalt tests show striking immaturity of visuo-motor functioning. Body image is usually very primitive. These children show disturbances in figure–background relationships, they are often hyperactive and have difficulty with patterning of motor and behavioural responses. They have, in fact, trouble at every level of integration . . . . maturation is largely a process of integration and differentiation. The child of six and older whose perceptual, motor, visuo-motor and conceptual performance is still relatively primitive, the child who has trouble with structuralisation of behavioural patterns, is the one who is liable to run into difficulties when he is exposed to reading, which requires the smooth interplay of many facets of behaviour.

More detailed results of some 20 years of clinical research on these lines by De Hirsch and two colleagues are published in *Predicting Reading Failure* (1966) in which they offer a "Predictive Index" by which children likely to run into learning difficulties can be identified early. In this study, it is shown how children who lag severely in overall maturation can be predicted to fail academically and it is demonstrated that valid predictions of reading, spelling and writing achievement can be made by evaluating children's perceptual motor and language behaviour at early ages. In developing their findings, De Hirsch and her colleagues have used modern research and statistical tools, but they have supplemented their methods by drawing on many years of clinical experience, working with many varieties of language disturbance in young children.

If developmental dyslexia is as Critchley (1966) sees it, "a genetically determined constitutional delay in maturation, a specialized instance of cerebral immaturity and not typically an expression of minor brain damage", it is probable that these children would also be identified by De Hirsch's tests, designed to discover potential reading difficulties in young children. De Hirsch, however, claimed for her tests not only that they would discover the child who is liable to run into trouble with reading, but also that they indicate areas in which the child's performance lags and in this way provide a lead as to what specific techniques could be usefully used in future teaching of these children.

Two other books, though not specifically dealing with special learning disorders, merit mention here. These are *The Bender Gestalt Test for Young Children* and *Psychological Evaluation of Children's Human Figure Drawings*, both by Koppitz (1964 and 1968). In her book on the Bender Gestalt, Koppitz describes her research study, which was carefully designed to determine whether the Bender Test could be used to differentiate between brain-injured and non-brain-injured school children, ranging in age from 5 to 10 years. Her thoughtful discussion of the results of her research study, illustrated by vivid examples from children who contributed to the study, provides a valuable addition to the diagnostic tools available to the psychologist in this very difficult field of study.

In her *Psychological evaluation of Children's Human Figure Drawings*, Koppitz presents a study of brain injury and human figure drawings. She bases her findings on the drawings of 213 children, ranging in age from 6 to 12 years, all of whom had been diagnosed as brain-injured by a neurologist. These children had an I.Q. range of 42–138 and none of them had any gross motor impairment. In her careful discussion of the results which followed, Koppitz again illustrates vividly how, though a child's human figure drawing should never be used alone for a differential diagnosis, it can, as part of a battery of tests, effectively support a diagnosis, so that the presence of several significant items on a human figure drawing can serve to supplement other psychological, medical and social data.

The Concept of Readiness

Finally, one other book is worthy of notice. This is a study of *School Readiness* by Ilg and Ames (1965). In it, they describe a series of behaviour tests used at The Gesell Institute to assess "school readiness". The emphasis on work from the Gesell Institute has always been on developmental patterns.

Although this book is concerned with the wide variations in developmental levels of behaviour in normal children, it contains such an interesting detailed analysis of maturation and mental growth in young children that it provides a useful source of reference for a psychologist who is making a comparison between development of normal and neurodevelopmentally handicapped children his field of study.

Historical Survey, 1973

Since the first edition of this book was published the frontiers of our knowledge and understanding of these children whose specific learning disorders are thought to arise from neuro-developmental dysfunction have been widened in many directions. There has developed a more active interest in the problems raised by this subject by neurologists. An interesting example of the interest in this subject is presented as the account of a Conference on Minimal Brain Dysfunction held at the New York Academy of Sciences. The detailed report of the Conference is published under the title, Minimal Brain Dysfunction. The conference took place in co-operation with the American Institute of Child Health and Human Development and the National Institute of Neurological Diseases. The conference was mainly concerned with medical aspects of this problem but contains also some interesting papers on the relation of minimal dysfunction to educational handicaps. A paper by Katrina de Hirsch brings very much up to date the relation between early language development and Minimal Brain Dysfunction.

The problem of reading disability still engages the interest of educationists as well as neurologists. MacDonald Critchley, working in England has published an extended revision of his work *The Dyslexic Child* and Naidoo has published her account of the Five Year Research project carried out under the auspices of the Invalid Children's Aid Association at the Word Blind Centre, London.

Perhaps the most stimulating and instructive contribution to the problems of identification of pre-school children likely to have reading problems in school is the book by Jansky and de Hirsch on *Preventing Reading Failure*. This is a continuation of their study published earlier under the title *Predicting Reading Failure*.

The relation of learning to perceptuo-motor disabilities in children is brought up to date in Wedell's study recently published.

The importance of the contribution of language to children's learning continues to remain in the forefront of interest. A very full report of the Conference sponsored by the Spastics Society is published in *Children with Delayed Speech*, edited by Rutter and Martin. Many of the papers reported here are relevant to the study of identification of learning disabilities in children.

Psychoeducational Evaluation of the Pre-School Child. A manual utilizing the Haeussermann Approach by Jedrysek, E., Klapper, Z., Pope, L., Wortis, J. This book provides an assessment procedure based on the techniques described in Haeussermann's book *Developmental Potential of Pre-School Children* (see Bibliography). This should be a most valuable addition to understanding of learning problems of pre-school children for teachers, paediatricians and psychologists.

Bibliography

ANTHONY, E. J. and BENE, E. (1957) Family relations test: a technique for the objective assessment of the child's family relations, *J. Men. Sci.*, **103**, 541–55.

ABERCROMBIE, M. L. J. (1964) Perceptual and visuo-motor disorders in cerebral palsy, *Little Club Clinics in Developmental Medicine*, No. 11.

ABERCROMBIE, M. L. J., GARDINER, P. A., HANSEN, E., JONCKHEERE, J., LINDON, R. L., SOLOMON, G. and TYSON, M. C. (1964) Visual perceptual and visuo-motor impairments in physically handicapped children, *Perceptual and Motor Skills, Monograph Supplement* 3, vol. V, No. 18, 1964.

ABRAVANEL, E. (1968) The Development of Intersensory Patterning with Regard to Selected Spatial Dimensions, *Monograph of Society for Research in Child Development*, No. 118, vol. 33, No. 2.

ALBITRECCIA, S. I. (1958) Recognition and Treatment of Disturbance of Body Image, *Cerebral Palsy Bulletin* vol. I, No. 4.

ALBITRECCIA, S. I. (1959) Treatment of disorders of the body image, *Spastics Quarterly*, **8**, (3) 30–32.

ANASTASI, A. (1961) *Psychological Testing*, 2nd ed., Macmillan, New York.

ARKELL, H. B. (1966) The Edith Norrie Letter Case, *I.C.A.A. Word Blind Bulletin*, **1** (5), Spring.

BARRY, H. (1961) *The Young Aphasic Child. Evaluation and Training*, Published by the Alexander Graham Bell Association for the Deaf, the Volta Bureau, Washington, D.C.

BAX, M. and MACKEITH, R. (Eds.) (1962) Minimal Cerebral Dysfunction, *Little Club Clinics in Developmental Medicine*, No. 10.

BAYLEY, N. (1943) Mental Growth during the First Three Years in *Child Behaviour and Development*, McGraw-Hill, New York.

BAYLEY, N. (1969) Bayley Scales of Infant Development: Manual, Psychological Corporation, New York.

BAYLEY, N. (1966) *The Two-year-old*, published by the Durham Educational Improvement Programme.

BENDER, L. (1938) *A Visual Motor Gestalt Test. Its Clinical Use*, Am. Orthopsychiatric Assoc. Research Monograph, No. 3.

BENDER, L. (1949) Psychological problems of children with organic brain disease, *Am. J. Orthopsychiatry*, **19** (3), July 1949.

BENDER, L. (1959) *Psychopathology of Children with Organic Brain Disorders*, Chas. C. Thomas.

BENDER, L. and SILVER, A. M. (1948) Body image problems of the brain injured child, *J. Social Issues*, Fall edition.

BENTON, A. L. (1959) *Right-Left Discrimination and Finger Localisation*, Hoeber, New York.

BERNSTEIN, B. (1960) Language and social class, *Brit. J. Sociol.* **11**, 271–6.

BERNSTEIN, B. (1961) Social structure, language and learning, *Educational Research*, **3** (3), June 1961.

BIRCH, H. G. (Ed.) (1964) *Brain Damage in Children. The Biological and Social Aspects*, Williams & Wilkins, Baltimore.

BIRCH, H. G. and BELMONT, L. (1965) Auditory-visual integration in brain damaged and normal children, *Dev. Med. Child Neurol.* **7**, 135–144.

BIRCH, H. G. and LEFFORD, A. (1963) Intersensory Development in Children, *Monograph of the Society for Research in Child Development*, No. 89, vol. 28, No. 5.

BORTNER, M. and BIRCH, H. G. (1962) Perceptual and perceptual-motor dissociation in Cerebral Palsy. *J. Nerv. Ment. Dis.* **134**, 103–8.

BOWLBY, J. (1951) *Maternal Care, Mental Health*, Geneva World Health Organisation, Monograph Series No. 2.

BOWLEY, A. (1969) Reading Difficulty with Minor Neurological Dysfunction. A Study of Children in Junior Schools. *Develop. Med. Child Neurol.* Vol. 11, 493–503.

BRAIN, R. (1961) *Speech Disorders, Aphasia, Apraxia and Agnosia*, Butterworth, London.

BROTTMAN, M. A. (Ed.) (1968) Language Remediation for the Disadvantaged Pre-School Child, *Monograph for Research in Child Dev.*, No. 124, vol. 33, No. 8.

BUHLER, C. (1945) *From Birth to Maternity*, Kegan Paul, London.

CALDWELL, E. M. (1956) *A Case of Spatial Inability in a Cerebral Palsied Child*, British Council for the Welfare of Spastics, No. 89, vol. 28, No. 5.

CARDWELL, VIOLA E. (1956) *Cerebral Palsy. Advances in Understanding and Care*, Assoc. for the Aid of Crippled Children.

CATTELL, Psyche (1960) *The Measurement of Intelligence of Infants and Young Children*, The Psychological Co-operation, New York, N.Y.

CHIEF MEDICAL OFFICER (1961 and 2, 1964 and 5) *Report on the Health of the School Child*, H.M.S.O.

CLARKE, A. D. B. (1961) Minimal Cerebral Palsy, Letter in *Cerebral Palsy Bulletin*, **3** (5), October.

CLARKE, A. D. B. (1966) *Recent Advances in the Study of Subnormality*, National Association for Mental Health.

CLEMENTS, S. D. (1966) *Minimal Brain Dysfunction in Children Phase One of a Three-Phase Project*, N.I.N.D.S. Monograph No. 3, U.S. Dept. of Health, Education and Welfare.

CORAH, N. L., ANTHONY, E. J., PAINTER, P., STEIN, J. and THURSTON, D. (1965) Effect of Perinatal Anoxia after Seven Years. *Psychol. Monogr.* No. 596, vol. 79, No. 3, A.P.A. Inc.

CRITCHLEY, M. (1961) Inborn Reading Disorders of Central Origin. Doyne Memorial Lecture, *Trans. Ophal. Soc. (U.K.)* **81**, 459.

CRITCHLEY, M. (1964) *Developmental Dyslexia*, Heinemann Medical Books Ltd. Second and augmented edition (1970).

CRITCHLEY, M. (1966) Is Developmental Dyslexia the Expression of Minor Cerebral Damage, *Clinical Proceedings*, Children's Hospital, Washington, D.C., **22** (8), September, 1966.

CRONBACH, Lee J. (1960) *Essentials of Psychological Testing*, 2nd edn., Harper & Row, New York.

CRUICKSHANK, W. M. (Ed.) (1966) *The Teacher of Brain-Injured Children. A discussion of the Bases of Competency.* Syracuse University Special Educational and Rehabilitation Monograph Series 7, Syracuse University Press.

CRUICKSHANK, W. M. (1968) *Educational Implications of Psychopathology in Brain-Injured Children. An Assessment of the Cerebral Palsied Child for Education*, published by Spastics Society in association with Heinemann Ltd.

CRUICKSHANK, W. M., BICE, H. V. and WALLEN, H. E. (1957) *Perception in Cerebral Palsy: a study in figure background relationship*, Syracuse University Press.

CRUICKSHANK, W. M., BENTZEN, F. A., RATZEBURG, F. H. and TANNHAUSER, M. T. (1961) *A Teaching Method for Brain-injured and Hyperactive Children*, Syracuse University Press.

DAVIE, R., BUTLER, N. and GOLDSTEIN, H. (1972) *From Birth to Seven*, Longman in association with National Children's Bureau.

DE HIRSCH, KATRINA (1957) Tests designed to discover potential reading difficulties at the six-year-old level, *Am. J. Orthopsychiatry* **27** (3), July 1957.

DE HIRSCH, KATRINA (1961) Studies in Tachyphemia: a diagnosis of developmental language disorders. LOGOS. **4** (1), 3–9 (April 1961).

DE HIRSCH, KATRINA (1963a) Psychological correlates of the reading process, *Bulletin of the Orton Society*, **13**.

DE HIRSCH, KATRINA (1963b) Concepts related to normal reading processes and their application to reading pathology, *J. Gen. Psychol.* **102**, 277–85.

DE HIRSCH, K., JANSKY, J. J., LANGFORD, WM. S. (1966) *Predicting Reading Failure*, Harper & Row, New York.

DELACATO, C. H. (1963) *Diagnosis and Treatment of Speech and Reading Problems*, published by Ch. C. Thomas.

DE LA CRUZ, FELIX F., FOX, BERNARD H. and ROBERTS, RICHARD H. (Eds.) *Minimal Brain Dysfunction*, The New York Academy of Sciences (1973).

DENHOFF, E. and ROBINAULT, I. (1960) *Cerebral Palsy and Related Disorders*, McGraw-Hill.

DOEHRING, D. G. (1968) *Patterns of Impairment in Specific Reading Disability*, Indiana University Press, Bloomington, Indiana.

DOLPHIN, J. E. and CRUICKSHANK, W. M. (1951a) The figure–background relationship in children with cerebral palsy, *J. Clin. Psychol.* **7**, 228–31.

DOLPHIN, J. E. and CRUICKSHANK, W. M. (1951b) Visuo-motor perception in children with cerebral palsy, *Quart. J. Child Behaviour*, **3**, 198–209.

DOLPHIN, J. E. and CRUICKSHANK, W. M. (1951c) Pathology of concept formation in children with cerebral palsy, *Am. J. Ment. Defic.* **56**, 386–92.

DOLPHIN, J. E. and CRUICKSHANK, W. M. (1952) Tactual motor perception of children with cerebral palsy, *J. Personal.* **20**, 466–71.

DUNSDON, M. (1951) *The Educability of Cerebral Palsied Children*, National Foundation for Educ. Research, Newnes Educ. Publ. Co., London.

DUNSING, J. D. and KEPHART, N. C. (1965) Motor Generalisations in Space and Time in *Learning Disorders*, vol. I, Special Child Publications, Seattle Seguin School Inc., Seattle, U.S.A.

ERNHART, C. B., GRAHAM, FRANCES K. and THURSTON, D. (1960) Relationship of neonatal apnea to development at three years, *A.M.A. Archives of Neurology*, **34**, 504–10.

ERNHART, CLAIRE B., GRAHAM, F. K., EICHMAN, P. L., MARSHALL, JOAN M. and THURSTON, D. (1963) Brain Injury in the Pre-School Child. Some Developmental Considerations. Comparisons of Brain Injured and Normal Children, *Psychol. Monogr.*, No. 574, vol. 77, No. 11.

FANTZ, R. L. (1966) Pattern discrimination and selective attention as determinants of perceptual development from birth, *Perceptual Development in Children*, Edited by Kidd, A. J. and Rivoire, J. L., University of London Press.

FINK, MAUD, BENDER, M. B. (1953) Perception of simultaneous tactile stimuli in normal children, *Neurology* **3**, 27–34 (1953).

FLAVELL, J. F. (1963) *The Developmental Psychology of Jean Piaget*, Van Nostrand, U.S.A.

FLOYER, E. B. (1955) *A Psychological Study of a City's Cerebral Palsied Children*, British Council for the Welfare of Spastics, London.

FRANCIS-WILLIAMS, J. M. (1964) Understanding and Helping the Distractible Child. *Learning Problems of the Cerebral Palsied*, Report of Oxford Study Group, Spastics Society.

FRANCIS-WILLIAMS, J. M. (1965) Special educational problems of children with minimal cerebral dysfunctions, *Spastics Quarterly*, vol. 14, No. 2.

FRANCIS-WILLIAMS, J. M. (1968) *Rorschach with Children*, Pergamon Press, pp. 101–9.

FRANCIS-WILLIAMS, J. M. (1969) Early recognition of pre-school children who are likely to have specific learning difficulties, *Planning for Better Learning*, Clinics in Developmental Medicine, No. 33. published by Spastics Society and Heinemann's Medical Press.

FRANKLIN, A. W. (Ed.) (1965) *Children with Communication Problems*, Pitman Medical Publishing Co., London.

FROSTIG, MARIANNE (1968) Testing as a Basis for Educational Therapy in *Assessment of the Cerebral Palsied Child for Education*, edited by Loring Spastics Soc. Heinemann.

FROSTIG, M., LEFEVER, D. W. and WHITTESLEY, J. (1961) Developmental test of visual perception for evaluating normal and neurologically handicapped children, *Perceptual and Motor Skills*, **12**, 383–94.

FROSTIG, M., MASLOW, P., LEFEVER, D. W. and WHITTESLEY, J. (1964) *The Marianne Frostig Developmental Test of Visual Perception*, Palo Alto, California: Consulting Psychologists Press.

FURTH, H. G. (1963) *Language and the Development of Thinking*, Report at Int. Congress on Education of the Deaf.

FURTH, H. G. (1966) *Thinking without Language. Psychological Implications of Deafness*, Collier-Macmillan Ltd.

GESELL, ARNOLD et al. (1940) *The First Five Years of Life*, Harper, New York.

GESELL, ARNOLD and AMATRUDA, C. S. (1941) *Developmental Diagnosis*, Hamish Hamilton Medical Books,

GESELL, A., ILG, F. L. and BULLIS (1949) *Vision: its development in infant and child*, Hoeber Inc., New York.

GHENT, LILA (1956) Perception of overlapping and embedded figures by children of different ages. *Am. J. Psychol.* **69** (4), 575–87 (December 1956).

GHENT, LILA (1961) Form and its orientation: a child's-eye view, *Am. J. Psychol.* **74** (2), 177–90 (June 1961).

GOLDFARB, W. (1955) Emotional and Intellectual Consequences of Psychologic Deprivation in Infancy: a Re-evaluation. Hoch, P. and Zelbin, J. (Eds.) *Psychopathology of Childhood*, Grune & Stratton, New York.

GOLDSTEIN, K. and SCHEERER, M. (1941) Abstract and concrete behaviour. *Psychol. Monogr.* vol. 53, No. 2.

GORDON, N. (1964) The Concept of Central Deafness in *The Child Who does not Talk*, Clinics in Developmental Medicine. No. 13 published by Spastics Society and Heinemann.

GORDON, N. (1964) The anatomy and physiology of the body image in childhood, *Dev. Med. Child Neurol.*, **6**, 641–4.

GORDON, N. (1966) Are these the Clumsy Children? Paper read to the Fifth International Conference, Spastics Society.

GRAHAM, D. (1965) The Contribution of Madame Stella Albitreccia in *Teaching the Cerebral Palsied Child*, edited by Loring, J. published by Spastics Society and Heinemann.

GRAHAM, F. K., BERMAN, P. W. and ERNHART, C. B. (1960) Development in pre-school children of the ability to copy forms, *Child Dev.* **31**, 339–59.

GRAHAM–ERNHART BLOCK SORT TEST MANUAL (1963) Published by American National Institute of Neurological Disease and Blindness, Perinatal Research Branch.

GRAHAM, F. K., ERNHART, C. B., THURSTON, D. and CRAFT, M. (1962) Development three years after perinatal anoxia and other potentially damaging newborn experiences, *Psychol. Monogr.* vol. 76, No. 3.

GRAHAM, F. K., ERNHART, C. B., CRAFT, M. and BERNAN, P. W. (1963) Brain injury in the pre-school child, some developmental considerations. Performance of normal children, *Psychol. Monogr.* vol. 77, No. 10.

HAEUSSERMANN, E. (1956) Estimating developmental potential of pre-school children with brain lesions, *Am. J. Ment. Defic.* **61** (1), 170–80.

HAEUSSERMANN, E. (1958) *Developmental Potential of Pre-School Children. An Evaluation of Intellectual, Sensory and Emotional Functioning*, Grune & Stratton Inc.

HALLGREN, BERTIL (1950) *Specific Dyslexia*, Clinical and Genetic Study, Copenhagen.

HANSEN, E. (1966) Personal communication.

HARKER, J. A. (1966) Personal communication.

HARRIS, D. B. (1963) *Children's Drawings as Measures of Intellectual Maturity*, Harcourt, Brace & World Inc.

HEBB, D. O. (1949) *Organisation of Behaviour. A Neuropsychological Theory*, John Wiley.

HELLMUTH, J. (Ed.) (1965) *Learning Disorders*, vol. 1. Special Child Publications, Seattle Seguin School, Inc., Seattle, U.S.A.

HERMANN, K. (1959) *Reading Disability*, Munksgaard, Copenhagen.

HINSHELWOOD, J. (1917) *Congenital Word Blindness*, Lewis, London.

HOLT, K. S. and REYNELL, J. K. (1967) *Assessment of Cerebral Palsy*, vol. II, Lloyd-Luke, London.

HONZIK, M. P. (1960) The Pattern of Mental Test Performance in Infants Suspected of Suffering Brain Injury, paper given at Am. Psych. Assoc., Chicago, September.

HONZIK, M. P. *et al.* (1965) Birth record assessments and test performance at eight months, *Am. J. Dis. Childhood*, **109**, 416–26.

ILG, F. L., AMES, L. B. (1965) *School Readiness. Behaviour Tests used at the Gesell Institute*, published by Harper & Row, New York.

ILLINGWORTH, R. S. (1958) Ed. *Recent Advances in Cerebral Palsy*, Churchill, London.

ILLINGWORTH, R. S. (1960) *The Development of the Infant and Young Child, Normal and Abnormal*, Edinburgh, Livingstone.

ILLINGWORTH, R. S. (1964) *The Normal School Child*, Heinemann Medical Books Ltd., London, pp. 20–24.

INGRAM, T. T. S. (1964) Late and Poor Talkers in *The Child Who Does Not Talk*, edited by Renfrew, C. and Murphy, K., Clinics in Developmental Medicine, No. 13. Spastics Society and Heinemann Medical Books Ltd.

JANSKY, JEANNETTE and DE HIRSCH, KATRINA (1972) *Preventing Reading Failure*, Harper & Row, New York.

JOHNSON, D. and MYKLEBUST, HELMER (1965) Dyslexia in Childhood in *Learning Disorders*, vol. I. Special Child Publications, Seattle Seguin School Inc., Seattle, U.S.A.

JOHNSON, D. and MYKLEBUST, HELMER (1967) *Learning Disabilities. Educational Principles and Practices*, Grune & Stratton, New York.

KEPHART, N. C. (1960) *The Slow Learner in the Classroom*, Chas. E. Merrill Books Inc., Columbus, Ohio.

KNOBLOCH, H. and PASAMANICK, B. (1959) Syndrome of minimal cerebral damage in infancy, *J. Amer. Med. Assoc.* **170**, 1384.

KNOBLOCH, H. and PASAMANICK, B. (1960) The developmental behavioural approach to the neurologic examination in infancy, *Child Development*, **33**, 181–98.

KOPPITZ, E. M. (1964) *The Bender Gestalt Test for Young Children*, Grune & Stratton, New York.

KOPPITZ, E. M. (1968) *Psychological Evaluation of Children's Human Figure Drawings*, Grune & Stratton, New York.

LANDRETH, CATHERINE (1967) *Early Childhood Behaviour and Learning*, Alfred A. Knoff, New York.

LANDRETH, CATHERINE (1972) *Pre-school Learning and Teaching*, Harper & Row.

LE BORNE, GHISLAINE, OF BRUSSELS (1965) A training method for reducing perceptual difficulties, *Spastics News*, vol. XI. No. IX, September 1965.

LEHTINEN, L. E. (1955) *Preliminary Conclusions affecting Education of Brain-Injured Children. Psychopathology and Education of the Brain-Injured Child*, Vol. II by Strauss, A. A. and Kephart, Newell C., Grune & Stratton, New York.

LUNZER, E. A. (1959) Intellectual development in the play of young children. *Educ. Rev.* XI (3), November 1959.

LURIA, A. R. (1961) *The Role of Speech in the Regulation of Normal and Abnormal Behaviour*, Pergamon, London.

LURIA, A. R. and YUDOVICH, F. L. (1959) *Speech and the Development of Mental Processes in the Child*, Staples, London.

MCCARTHY, J. J. and KIRK, S. A. (1961) *Illinois Test of Psycholinguistic Abilities*, University of Illinois, Urbana, Illinois, U.S.A.

MCGINNIS, M. A. (1963) *Aphasic Children: Identification and Education by the Association Method;* Alexander Graham Bell Association for the Deaf, Washington.

MCGINNIS, M. A., KLEFFNER, F. R. and GOLDSTEIN, R. (1960) *Teaching Aphasic Children*, the Volta Burea, 1537 35th Street, Washington, D.C.

MONEY, JOHN (1962) Ed. *Reading Disability: Progress and Research Needs in Dyslexia*, Johns Hopkins Press, Baltimore.

MORLEY, M. E. (1957) *Development and Disorders of Speech in Childhood*, Livingstone, Edinburgh.

MYKLEBUST, H. R. (1964) *The Psychology of Deafness*, Grune & Stratton, New York.

NAIDOO, S. (1961) An investigation into some aspects of ambiguous handedness, M.A. Thesis, University of London.

NAIDOO, S. (1972) *Specific Dyslexia*, Pitman Publishing Corporation.

NEWSON, ELIZABETH (1955) The development of line figure discrimination in pre-school children, Ph.D. Thesis, University of Nottingham, May 1955.

NIELSEN, H. H. (1962) Visual motor functioning of cerebral palsied and normal children. *Nord. Psy. Kol.* **14**, 41–104.

NIELSEN, H. H. (1966) *A Psychological Study of Cerebral Palsied Children*, Munksgaard, Copenhagen.

NOOTEBOOM, W. E. (1968) *Some Psychological Aspects of the Choreateform Syndrome*, Royal Vangorcum Ltd., Assen, The Netherlands.

O'DOHERTY, N. J. (1963) Minor neurological damage in young infants, *Guy's Hospital Gazette*, **77**, 80.

ORTON, S. (1937) *Reading, Writing and Speech Problems in Children*, Chapman & Hall, London.

PAINE, RICHMOND S. (1962) Minimal chronic brain syndromes in children, *Dev. Med. Child Neurol.* **4**, 21–27.

PAINE, RICHMOND S. (1965) Organic neurological factors related to learning disorders, in *Learning Disorders* vol. 1, Special Child Publications, Seattle Seguin School Inc., Seattle, U.S.A.

PAINE, RICHMOND S. and OPPÉ, THOMAS E. (1966) *Neurological Examination of Children*, Clinics in Developmental Medicine Nos. 20 and 21.

PIAGET, J. (1950) *The Psychology of Intelligence*, London, Routledge & Kegan Paul.

PIAGET, J. (1951) *Play, Dreams and Imagination in Childhood*, Heinemann, London.

PIAGET, J. (1953) *The Origins of Intelligence in the Child*, Routledge & Kegan Paul, London.

PIAGET, J. (1955) *The Child's Construction of Reality*, Routledge & Kegan Paul, London.

PIAGET, J. and INHELDER, B. (1956) *The Child's Conception of Space*, Routledge & Kegan Paul, London.

PLOWDEN, B. (1968) *Children and their Primary Schools. A Report of the Central Advisory Council for Education (England)*, vol. 1. chap. 19, H.M.S.O., Providing for Children before Compulsory Education.

POND, D. (1960) Is there a syndrome of "brain damage" in children, *Cerebral Palsy Bulletin*, vol. 2, No. 4.

POND, D. (1967) Communication Disorders in Brain-Damaged Children. *Proc. Royal Soc. Med.* **60**, 343–8 (April).

PRECHTL, H. F. R. (1962) Reading difficulties as a neurological problem in childhood, in *Reading Disability*, edited by John Money, Johns Hopkins Press, Baltimore.

PRECHTL, H. F. R. and BEINTEMA, D. (1964) *The Neurological Examination of the Full Term Newborn Infant*, Clinics in Developmental Medicine No. 12 Spastics Soc. and Heinemann Medical Press.

PRECHTL, H. F. R. and STEMMER, J. C. (1962) Choreiform syndrome in children, *Dev. Med. Child Neurol.* **4**, 119–27.

PRINGLE, KELLMER, M. Seven-year-olds Who Cannot Read, Longmans in association with the National Bureau for Co-operation in Child Care (in preparation).

RAM, M. (1962) Some educational aspects of the visuo-spatial handicap in C.P. children. *Spastics Quarterly*, vol. 11. No. 1. March, 1962.

RAPPAPORT, SHELDON, R. (Ed.) (1964) *Childhood Aphasia and Brain Damage*, vol. 1. *A Definition*.

RAPPAPORT, SHELDON R. (1965) *Childhood Aphasia and Brain Damage*, vol. 11. *Differential Diagnosis*, Published for the Pathway School by Livingstone Publishing Co., Naberth, Pennsylvania.

RENFREW, C. (1964) Speech Therapy for Late and Poor Talkers. In *The Child Who does not Talk*, Clinics in Developmental Medicine No. 13. Spastics Society and Heinemann Medical Books Ltd.

REYNELL, J. (1969) Infant and Young Children's Language Scales, Manual and Test Material for Development Language Scales, published by the National Foundation for Educational Research, London.

RUTTER, M. (1968) The Concept of Dyslexia, Paper read at 6th International Study Group of Child Neurology and C.P., Oxford.

RUTTER, M. and MARTIN, J. A. M. (1972) *The Child with Delayed Speech. Clinics in Developmental Medicine No. 43*. Spastics International Medical Publications, Heinemann Medical Books Ltd.

RUTTER, M., TIZARD, J. and WHITMORE, K. (Eds.) (1970) *Education, Health and Behaviour*, Longman.

RUSSELL, W. R., (1958) Disturbances of the body image, *Cerebral Palsy Bulletin*, **4**, 7–8.

SCHAFFER, H. R. (1958) Objective observations of personality development in early infancy, *Brit. J. Med. Psychol.* **31**, 174–83.

SCHAFFER, H. R. (1963) Some issues for research in the study of attachment behaviour, in *Determinants of Infant Behaviour*. Vol. 11, edited by Foss, B. M., Methuen, London.

SCHAFFER, H. R. (1966) The onset of fear of strangers and the incongruity hypothesis, *J. Child Psychol. Psychiat.* **7** (2), 95.

SCHAFFER, H. R. and PARRY, M. H. (1969) Perceptual-motor behaviour in infancy as a function of age and stimulus familiarity, *Brit. J. Psychol.* **60** (1), 1–9.

SCHAFFER, H. R. (1971) *The Growth of Sociability*, Penguin Science of Behaviour Series.

SCHAIN, RICHARD J. (1972) *Neurology of Childhood Learning Disorders*, The Williams and Wilkins Co., Baltimore.

SCHONELL, F. E. (1958) Intelligence testing and educational problems and methods of teaching, in *Recent Advances in Cerebral Palsy*, edited by Illingworth R. S., Churchill, London.

SHERIDAN, M. D. (1958) *The Stycar Vision Test, The Stycar Hearing Test*, distributed by National Foundation for Educational Research, London.

SHERIDAN, M. D. (1961) The child's hearing for spoken language, *Cerebral Palsy Bulletin*, vol. 3, No. 1.

SHERIDAN, M. D. (1962) Mentally handicapped children, *Dev. Med. Child Neurol.*, **4**, 71–6.

SHERIDAN, M. D. (1964) Development of Auditory Attention and Language Symbols in Young Children, in *The Child Who Does Not Talk*. Clinics in Developmental Medicine No. 13 Spastics Soc. and Heinemann Med. Books Ltd.

SHERIDAN, M. D. (1968) Personal communication.

SPITZ, R. A. (1945) Hospitalism, in *Psychoanalytic Study of the Child*, vol.1, International Universities Press, New York.

STONE, F. H. (1961) Is there a syndrome of brain damage in children? *Cerebral Palsy Bulletin*, vol. 3, No. 1.

STOTT, L. H. and BALL, R. S. (1965) Infant and Pre-School Mental Tests: Review and Evaluation. *Monograph of Soc. for Research in Child Development*, No. 101, vol. 30, No. 3.

STRAUSS, A. A. and KEPHART, N. C. (1955) *Psychopathology and Education of the Brain-Injured Child*, vol. 2, Grune & Stratton, New York.

STRAUSS, A. A. and LEHTINEN, L. E. (1947) *Psychopathology and Education of the Brain-Injured Child*, vol. 1, Grune & Stratton, New York.

STROTHER, C. H. (1963) *Discovering, Evaluating, Programming for the Neurologically Handicapped Child with Special Attention to the Child with Minimal Brain Damage*, Nat. Society for Crippled Children.

STRUTSMAN, R. (1931) *Mental Measurement of Pre-School Children*, World Book Company, Yonkers on Hudson, New York.

STUART M. F. (1963) *Neurophysiological Insights into Teaching*, Pacific Book Publishers, Palo Alto, California.

TARNOPOK (1971) *Learning Disorders in Children; Diagnosis, Medication, Education*, Little Brown & Co. Chapter on *The Neurology of Learning Disabilities* by Philip R. Calanchini and Susan Struve Trout.

TAYLOR, EDITH MEYER (1959) *Psychological Appraisal of Children with Cerebral Defects*, Harvard University Press.

TERMAN, L. M. and MERRILL, M. A. (1937) *Measuring Intelligence*, Harrap, London.

TYSON, M. (1963) Pilot study of remedial visuomotor training, *Special Education*, vol. 52.

VERNON, M. D. (1962) *The Psychology of Perception*, Penguin Books.

VERNON, M. D. (1965) The development of perception, chap. V in *Modern Perspectives in Child Psychiatry*, edited by Howells, J. G., Oliver & Boyd.

VERNON, P. E. (1960) *Intelligence and Attainments Tests*, University of London Press.

VYGOTSKY, L. S. (1962) *Thought and Language*, Institute of Technology Press, Cambridge, Massachusetts.

WALTON, J. N., ELLIS, E. and COURT, S. D. M. (1962) Clumsy children: developmental apraxia and agnosia, *Brain* vol. 82, Part III, pp. 603–612.

WECHSLER, D. (1949) Wechsler Intelligence Scale for Children, Psychological Corporation, New York.

WECHSLER, D. (1967) Wechsler Pre-School and Primary Scale of Intelligence for Children aged 4 to 6½ years. Psychological Corporation, New York.

WEDELL, K. (1960a) Visual perception of cerebral palsy children, *J. Child Psychol. Psychiat.* **1**, pp. 215–227.

WEDELL, K. (1960b) Variations in perceptual ability among types of cerebral palsy, *Cerebral Palsy Bulletin* **2** (3), 149–157.

WEDELL, K. (1964a) Some Aspects of Perceptual-Motor Development in Young Children in *Learning Problems of the Cerebral Palsied*, The Spastics Society, London.

WEDELL, K. (1964b) Some Developmental Disorders of Speech in *Learning Problems of the Cerebral Palsied*, The Spastics Society, London.

WEDELL, K. (1965) Shape discrimination and shape copying: a pilot study on the effects of training children at 3¾ and 5¼ years, *Teaching the Cerebral Palsied Child*, edited by James Loring, Spastics Society.

WEDELL, K. (1966) Provision in Bristol for Children with Delayed Speech (personal communication).

WEDELL, K. (1973) *Learning and Perceptuo-motor Disabilities in Children.* John Wiley & Sons.

WEPMAN, J. M. (1958) Wepman Test of Auditory Discrimination. Chicago: Language Research Associates.

WILLIAMS, J. M. (1958) Some special learning difficulties of cerebral palsied children, *Cerebral Palsy Bulletin*, vol. I, No. 2.

WILLIAMS, J. M. (1961) Children who break down in Foster Homes: a psychological study of patterns of personality growth in grossly deprived children, *J. Child Psychol. Psychiat.*, Pergamon Press Ltd., pp. 5–20.

WILSON, M. (1966) *The Education of Brain-Injured Children in the United States of America*, published by the Greater London Council.

WILSON, M. (1966) Problems in Providing Special Education in *Early Childhood Autism*, edited by Wing, J. R. published by Pergamon Press.

WOODS, G. E. (1957) *Cerebral Palsy in Childhood*, Wright, Bristol.

WOODS, G. E. (1958) The development of body image, *Cerebral Palsy Bulletin* **1** (4), 9–11.

WOODWARD, M. (1959) The behaviour of idiots interpreted by Piaget's theory of sensori-motor developments, *Brit. J. Educ. Psychol.* **24**, 60–71.

WOODWARD, M. (1962) Application of Piaget's theory to the training of the subnormal, *J. of Ment. Subnorm.*, vol. 8, No. 1.

WOODWARD, M. (1965) Piaget's theory, chap. IV in *Modern Perspectives in Child Psychiatry*, edited by Howells, J. G., published by Oliver & Boyd.

WORSTER-DROUGHT, C. (1965) Disorders of speech in childhood, chap. XIV in *Modern Perspectives in Child Psychiatry*, edited by Howells, J. G., published by Oliver & Boyd.

YULE, W. (1966) University of London, Institute of Education (personal communication).

YULE, W. (1967) Predicting reading ages on Neale's analysis of reading ability, *British J. Educ. Psychology*, **37**, 252-255.

YULE, W., BERGER, M., BUTLER, S,. NEWHAM, V. and TIZARD, J. (1969) The W.P.P.S.I.: an empirical evaluation with a British sample, *Brit. J. Educ. Psychol.* vol. 39, Part 1, February 1969.

ZANGWILL, O. L. (1960) *Cerebral Dominance and its Relation to Psychological Function*, Oliver & Boyd, Edinburgh.

ZANGWILL, O. L. (1962) The Johns Hopkins dyslexia conference, *Dev. Med. Child Neurol.*, **4**, 205–209.

ZANGWILL, O. L. (1962) Dyslexia in relation to cerebral dominance, in *Reading Disability*, edited by John Money, Johns Hopkins Press, Baltimore.

Index

Accommodation process 18
Achievement Center for Children
    in Purdue University,
    Indiana 197
Aggression 162
Agnosia 201
Aide aux Enfants Paralyses Centre
    87
Anoxic hypotonia 80
Aphasia and aphasics 12–13, 14,
    81, 100–1, 147, 164, 193
Apraxia 201
Articulatory mechanisms,
    disorders of 12
Assimilation process 18
Association tests 113
Athetoids 6
Attachment behaviour 23
Attention span 73, 76
Auditory aphasia 138
Auditory decoding 113
Auditory imperception 81, 138, 205
Auditory memory 166
Auditory-vocal association test 113
Auditory-vocal automatic test 115
Auditory-vocal sequencing and
    visuo-motor 159
Autistic children 11, 101, 162

Barry's Evaluation and Training of
    the Young Aphasic Child
    164
Bayley Infant Mental and Motor
    Scales 27, 28
Behaviour development 28
Behaviour pattern 202
  and perceptual disorders 7–11

Behavioural assessment 35
Behavioural characteristics 168
Belmont Hospital 158
Bender Face-Hand-test 33, 38
Bender Gestalt test 110, 124, 126,
    145, 156, 208, 209
Bibliography 212
Binet Picture Vocabulary 33, 38
Blind pupils 150
Block sort test 32, 37, 60, 64, 67, 70,
    71, 78
Body concept 149
Body image 58, 59, 149
  concept 57
  delayed sense of 73
  development of 90
  disorders of 87
  disturbance 11
Body schema 149
Brain damage 3, 83, 192, 202
  diagnosis of 8
  effects of 8
  localization and extent of 6
  minimal 83, 164, 201–2
  symptoms of 8
Brain damage syndrome 147
Brain-damaged adults 193
Brain-damaged children 1, 4, 7, 9,
    27, 28, 59, 72, 73, 105–6, 109,
    124, 139, 142–3, 146–8, 151,
    169, 194–6, 199, 200
Brain-damaged child syndrome 194
Brain-injury ratings 33
Bristol Nursery School for Cerebral
    Palsied Children 90

Cattell Infant Intelligence Scale 32

Central nervous system 58, 142, 164
Cerebral dysfunction 168
Cerebral palsied children 5–7, 11, 28, 31, 64, 72, 86, 88, 99, 124, 136, 151, 172, 201
Cerebral palsy 2, 9, 12, 141
  differing types of 6
  minimal 9–11
Cheyne Walk School for Cerebral Palsied Children 158–9
Child guidance clinic 105, 187
Children's Hospital, Boston 99
  Philadelphia 202
  Washington D.C. 198–9
Chi-square test 56
Choreiform syndrome 200
Clumsiness 10, 64, 73, 79, 90
Clumsy children 9, 11, 89, 104, 129, 135, 157, 173, 201–5
Communication difficulties and disorders 162, 199
Concentration, capacity for 45, 49
Concentration development of 98
Concentration span 121
Concept formation 64
Concept test 32, 37, 70
Congenital auditory imperception 81, 138
Congenital word blindness 13, 14
Continuum of reproductive casualty 83
Copy-forms test 32, 35, 58, 60, 64, 67, 69, 78
Cove Schools 144, 196

Deaf children 71, 163
Deaf pupils 150
Deafness 11, 12, 25
  central 81, 138, 205
Decoding tests 113
Delayed Speech Unit 162
Delicate pupils 151
Demonstration-pilot study 142
Deprivation syndrome 21, 22
Deprived children 101
Development, deviations from normal 27–9

Developmental articulatory dyspraxia 129
Developmental diagnosis 192
Developmental dyslexia
  see Dyslexia
Developmental lag 5, 10
Developmental language scales 40–1
Developmental neurology 198–9
Developmental patterns 210
Developmental profile 147
Developmental Reading Programme Rehabilitation Centre 149
Developmental receptive and expressive dysphasia 12
Diagnosis 9, 14
  developmental 192
  differential 113–41
  educational 146–7
Diagnostic assessment 75, 106, 167, 204
Differential diagnosis
  case histories 119–41
  of linguistic ability 113–19
Digit repetition test 117
Disadvantaged children 101
Distractibility 7–8, 73, 98–100, 195
Draw-a-person test 58
"Dysarthric" children 12
Dyslexia 13–15, 133, 135, 139, 140, 165–6, 198, 206–8
Dysphasia 13, 100
Dyssymbolia 200

Early learning 16–29
Edith Edwards House School 162
Educational diagnosis 146–7
Educational therapy tests 148
Educationally subnormal children 150, 161, 163
E.E.G. abnormalities 199
E.E.G. record 164
Ego-centricity 70
Ego control impairment of 8
Ego development 148
Electronic devices 164
Emotional adjustment 33
Emotional deprivation 11

Emotional disorders 3, 141
Emotional disturbance 166
Emotional problems 162
Emotional relationships 101
Emotionally disturbed children 143
Encephalitis 166
Encoding tests 115
Endogenous retarded child 195
Epilepsy 2, 10
Epileptic pupils 150
Experimental schools 142, 146
Exercises, remedial 87–8
Exogenous retarded child 195
Eye-motor co-ordination 110
  and play materials 152

Family Relations Test 33
Fear of strangers 21–3
Figure–ground discrimination 10, 38, 195
Figure–ground disturbance 7
Figure–ground perception 109, 110
Figure–ground test 33
Figure–ground work-book 155
Follow-up studies 175–191
Form, perception of 93
Form constancy, perception of 110
Frostig Developmental Test of Visual Perception 33, 118, 133, 148, 156
Frustration, reaction to 121

Genetic conditions 135
Gerstmann's Syndrome 201
Gesell Institute 209–10
Global syndrome 21–2
Goldstein Scheerer Sticks test 156
Goodenough Drawing of a Man Scale 38
Goodenough–Harris scoring system 58
Graham and Kendall Memory for Designs Test 133
Guy's Hospital 47, 54, 178

Hand dominance 48

Handicapped children 86, 141, 150
  assessment of 75
Handicapped Pupils and Special Schools Regulations 1959 150
Head injuries 10
Head start class 157
Head start programmes 101
Hemiparesis 129
Hemiplegia 6, 27, 89
Hemiplegic children 28
Historical survey 192–210
Hospitalization, effect of 21, 22
Human figure drawings 209
Hydrocephalics 10
Hyperactive children 98, 142–4
Hyperactivity 147, 195
Hyperkinetic children 125
Hyperkinetic syndrome 204

Identification
  of children with learning disabilities 30–74, 77, 102–3
  of deviant development 16, 19, 21, 24, 27, 29
Illinois Psycho-linguistics Test 113, 133, 159
Infant development 17–18, 22–4, 27, 58, 86
Integration, poor capacity for 72–3
Intellectual functioning assessment of 107
Intellectual strengths and weaknesses tests for 109–19
Intelligence 32
Intelligence scale, new English 118
Intelligence test results 56
Intelligence tests 32, 170
Inter-sensory integration 28
Inter-sensory-patterning 72
Intuitive thought period of 20–9
Isle of Wight Survey 172, 206

John Horniman School 161, 163

Kohs Goldstein Blocks test 156

Language   25, 66, 71, 72
  assessment of receptive and
      expressive aspects   41
  basic   102
  expressive   25, 44
  inner   25, 26
  receptive   25
Language ability   20
Language development   24–6, 28,
    35, 40, 50
  measurement of   113
  retarded   73
  social differences in 101
Language disabilities and disorders
    3, 11–13, 81–5, 100–3, 108,
    138, 159, 163, 164, 166, 193,
    194, 205–9
Language remediation programmes
    101
Language scales, developmental 40–1
Learning disabilities and disorders
    1–4, 30, 161, 170
Learning processes   197
Learning programmes, structured
    147
Learning theory   171
Line figure discrimination   91
Linguistic ability, differential
    diagnosis of   113–19
L–M Revision of Stanford–Binet
    Scale   77, 107
Lobectomies   10

Maladjusted pupils   150
Maladjustment ratings   33
Manipulation of spatial relationships
    5, 11
Manor Hospital, Epsom   161
Manual dexterity   90
Mark-the-car test   33, 38
Maturational disturbances   1, 2, 3,
    104–5, 108
Maturational lag   110, 135, 173
McGinnis's Association Method
    147, 164
Memory test   133
Mental retardation   141

Mentally subnormal children   84–5,
    100–1, 160–1
Minimal Brain Dysfunction in
    Children 142
Minimal Brain Dysfunction
    Syndrome   203, 210
Mongoloid children   102
Montgomery County Public School
    Department of Special Educa-
    tion   143
Moor House School   161, 163
Mother, acceptance of child   45
Mother and child relationship   76
Motor co-ordination   64
Motor co-ordination impairment
    89–98
Motor-co-ordination test   32
Motor development   28, 73
Motor disability   78–81
Movement   73
  development of   64

National Bureau for Co-operation
    in Child Care   173
National Foundation for Educa-
    tional Research   173
Neale Analysis of Reading Ability
    126, 131, 156, 179, 181–8
Neurodevelopmental learning
    disorders   1, 30, 173
Neurological impairment   32, 46–8,
    79, 88, 104–5, 108, 138, 139
Neurological organization   149
Neurologically handicapped chil-
    dren   76, 110, 151, 160
Neuro-psychologists   198
Newcastle Sample   163
North Western University   164
Nursery school   86, 90, 92, 99, 100,
    103, 162, 164, 174
  Tavistock Clinic   31, 34, 40, 59

Object sorting test   70
Organic impairment   5, 105, 135,
    138, 139
Organic pattern   2

Orientation disturbance 10
Overlapping and embedded figures, perception of 95–8

Paediatric Language Disorder Clinic 207
Partially deaf pupils 150
Partially sighted pupils 150
Pathway School 147
Perception
    definition 4
    of form 93
    of form constancy 110
    of overlapping and embedded figures 95–8
    of position in space 110
    of spatial relations 24, 86, 110
    of strangers 23
Perceptual ability levels 90–1
Perceptual development 31, 35, 40
Perceptual discrimination 92
Perceptual disorders 6–11, 85–9, 135, 196–8
Perceptual-motor battery 33
Perceptual-motor development 92
Perceptual-motor tests 32
Perceptual training 148–9
Percy Hedley Cerebral Palsy School 157
Perinatal anoxia 32, 83–4, 127
Peripheral-distraction sub-test 33
Personality assessment 35
Physically handicapped children 152
Physically handicapped pupils 150
Pilot School for the Brain Injured Child 146
Pilot studies 34–45, 142
Play behaviour 19, 20
Play exercises and play materials 152–6
Plowden Committee 172
Plowden Report 103, 171, 174
Post-natal apnœa 84
Pre-conceptual period 19–20, 26
Predictive Index 208
Pregnancy 166

Pre-school children 170, 173, 175, 207
    experiments in helping 85–103
Pre-school clinic 164
Programmed learning 171
Projective techniques 35
Psychiatric disturbances 199
Psychological assessment 134, 158, 168–70
Psychological disturbances 11
Psychological tests 10, 32, 50, 167, 168, 169, 200
Psychologist's contribution 105–7, 167–70
Psychologist's tools 106
Psychoneurological disabilities 1

Rating scales 45, 48–9, 50, 56
Reading Ability, Neale Test of 156
Reading difficulties and disabilities 13–15, 100, 104, 139, 140, 159, 166, 194, 207–9
    case histories 119–41
Recognition of forms 5
"Reflex schemata" 23–4
Remedial teaching, training and techniques 87–8, 108, 136, 137, 151, 152, 155, 156, 160, 198
Research
    design 46–8
    historical survey 192–210
    projects 172
    testing, observations arising from 57–74
Restlessness 7–8, 124–5
Results of follow-up tests 180–9
Reynell's tests 72, 81, 82, 181–9
Right–left discrimination 10, 124, 149
Rorschach 33

St. Luke's Hospital, Guildford 46, 47, 178
Schonell's Graded Word Spelling Test 131
School-age children 104–41

School of Educational Therapy,
    Los Angeles 148
School medical officer 2, 105, 165
School performance 176
    poor 1–2, 10
School psychological service 105,
    176
School psychologist 2
School Readiness 192
School visits 176
Schools
    experimental 142, 146
    special 157
Self-concept 38, 59, 78
Self-portrait 56–8, 124
Self-portrait test 59–63
Sensori-motor period 17–19, 27
Sensori-motor training 148
Sensory deprivation 22, 100
Sensory hyperactivity 98
Sensory training 86
Sequencing tests 117
Sex differences 56, 71
Shape copying 92
Shape discrimination 92
Shape perception 24
Social class
    differences and verbal tests 54
    distribution 54
    effect of 45
Social development 21–3
Social differences in
        language development 101
Social factors 105
Sonoma State Hospital 102
Spastics 6, 27
Spatial perception 24, 86, 110
Spatial relationships 5, 11, 110, 148
Special education 170
Special schools 157
Speech 27, 66
    integration 66
Speech defective unit 162
Speech development 11, 12
    delayed 73, 131
Speech difficulties and disorders
        12, 52, 82, 100–3, 150, 163, 166
Speech therapy 82, 137, 162, 184

Split-half reliability with Spearman
        correction of the Reynell tests
        45
Stanford–Binet Intelligence Scale
        32, 38, 91
    L–M Revision of 77, 107
Stanford–Binet test 5
Strangers
    fear of 21–3
    perception of 23
Strauss syndrome 126, 146
Strephosymbolia 166, 194
Stress effects 140
Study conferences 172
Stycar tests 130
Syndrome of minimal cerebral
        damage 83

Tactual-localization test 33, 38,
        56–8
Tavistock Clinic nursery school 31,
        34, 40, 59
Teachers, special 152
Teaching experiments and methods
        142–67, 198
    guides to 109–19
Test results, summary of 57
Tests
    choice and use of 76
    surveys of 75

Understanding
    development of 21
    growth of 26
University, North Western 164
University of Wisconsin 164

Verbal ability, test of 38–45
Verbal comprehension assessment of
        41
Verbal–performance differences 108
Verbal tests, and social class differ-
        ences 54
Verbalization 64–70
Vineland Scale of Social Maturity
        145

Visual aphasia   138
Visual perception
  development of   23–4
  developmental test of   109–13
  teaching programme   148
Visual-perceptual difficulties and
    disorders   3–11, 152
Visual perceptual processes   73
Visuo-motor association tests   113
Visuo-motor difficulties and
    disorders   3–11, 152
Visuo-motor perceptual ability   28
Visuo-motor performance   156
Visuo-motor sequencing test   118
Visuo-motor skills   149
  disorderly development of   85–9
Visuo-motor training   152
Visuo-spatial disability and disorders
    5, 28, 35, 78–81, 108, 196–8
Visuo-spatial perception   73, 91
Visuo-spatial tests   6
Vocabulary scale   32

Wechsler Intelligence Scale for
    Children   10, 107–8, 121, 126,
    131, 133, 134, 156, 178, 181–6
  vocabulary sub-test   84, 181–6
Wechsler Pre-school and Primary
    Scale of Intelligence   10, 28,
    79, 81, 107–8
Wepman Test of Auditory Discrimi-
    nation   118
Wisconsin, University of   164
Withdrawal   162
Word-Blind Centre   165
Word-blind children   165
Word-blind Institute, Copenhagen
    166
Word-blindness   140, 194
Word-deafness   138

Zazzo's adaptations
  of Bender Gestalt test   156
  of Kohs Goldstein Blocks test
    156